Business Result

SECOND EDITION

Advanced *Teacher's Book*

Rachel Appleby,
Heidi Grant &
Lynne White

OXFORD

UNIVERSITY PRESS

OXFORD
UNIVERSITY PRESS

Great Clarendon Street, Oxford, OX2 6DP, United Kingdom

Oxford University Press is a department of the University of Oxford.
It furthers the University's objective of excellence in research, scholarship,
and education by publishing worldwide. Oxford is a registered trade
mark of Oxford University Press in the UK and in certain other countries

First published in 2018

2024

10 9 8 7 6 5 4

No unauthorized photocopying

ISBN: 978 0 19 473912 2   Book
ISBN: 978 0 19 473911 5   Pack

Printed in China

This book is printed on paper from certified and well-managed sources

ACKNOWLEDGEMENTS

Cover image: Getty Images/Monashee Frantz

Back cover photograph: Oxford University Press building/David Fisher

*The authors and publisher would like to thank Saïd Business School for their assistance
in producing the Viewpoint video interviews on the Teacher's Book DVD. In particular,
we would like to thank the following people for their time, assistance and expertise*:
Nazia Ali, Ahmed Abu Bakr, Lydia Darley, Louise Fitzgerald, Kathy Harvey,
Thomas Hellmann, Sophie Kin Seong, Georgia Lewis, Tim Morris, Ana María
Ñungo, Thomas Pilsworth, Andy Poole, Josie Powell, Nancy Puccinelli, Hiram
Samel, Andrew Stephen, Breanne Svehla, Jonathan Trevor, Peter Tufano, John
Walugembe.

Contents

Introduction 4–7

1 Connections 8–14

2 Careers 15–21

3 Change 22–27

Viewpoint 1 Dealing with change 28–29

4 Risk 30–36

5 Teamwork 37–43

6 Progress 44–48

Viewpoint 2 Ethical consumption 49–50

7 Learning 51–57

8 Performance 58–64

9 Resources 65–70

Viewpoint 3 Business education 71

10 Leadership 72–77

11 Values 78–84

12 Persuasion 85–89

Viewpoint 4 Leading the future 90–91

Practice file answer key 92–96

Introduction

The course

Who is *Business Result Second Edition* for?

Business Result Second Edition is a comprehensive multi-level course in business English suitable for a wide range of learners. The main emphasis is on *enabling* your students, helping them to communicate more effectively in their working lives.

In-work students

Unlike many business English courses, *Business Result Second Edition* addresses the language and communication needs of employees at all levels of an organization, who need to use English at work. It recognizes that the business world is truly international, and that many people working in a modern, global environment spend much of their time doing everyday tasks in English – communicating with colleagues and work contacts by phone, via email, and in a range of face-to-face situations, such as formal and informal meetings/discussions, and various planned and unplanned social encounters. The course contains topics and activities that allow the students to participate in a way that is relevant to them, whatever their level in their company or organization.

Pre-work learners

Business Result Second Edition can also be used with pre-work learners at college level. The course covers a variety of engaging topics over the 12 units, so students without much work experience will receive a wide-ranging overview of the business world, as well as acquiring the key communication skills they will need in their future working lives. Each unit in this *Teacher's Book* contains suggestions for adapting the material to the needs of these students.

One-to-one teaching

Many of the activities in the book are designed for use with groups of students, but they can also be easily adapted to suit a one-to-one teaching situation. Notes in the *Teacher's Book* units offer suggestions and help with this.

What approach does *Business Result Second Edition* take?

Business Result Second Edition helps students communicate in English in real-life work situations. The priority at all times is on enabling them to do so more effectively and with confidence. The target language in each unit has been carefully selected to ensure that students will be equipped with genuinely useful, transferable language that they can take out of the classroom and use immediately in the workplace.

The course recognizes that, with so many businesses now being staffed by people of different nationalities, there is an increasing trend towards using English as the language of internal communication in many organizations. As well as learning appropriate language for communicating externally – with clients or suppliers, for example – students are also given the opportunity to practise in situations that take place within an organization, such as giving a report, making arrangements and taking part in meetings.

The main emphasis of the course is on the students speaking and trying out the target language in meaningful and authentic ways; it is expected that a large proportion of the lesson time will be spent on activating students' interest and encouraging them to talk. The material intentionally takes a communicative, heads-up approach, maximizing the amount of classroom time available to focus on and practise the target language. However, you will also find that there is plenty of support in terms of reference notes, written practice and review material.

The syllabus is essentially communication-driven. The topics in each of the 12 units have been chosen because of their relevance to modern business and the world of work. Vocabulary is presented in realistic contexts with reference to real companies or organizations. Grammar is also a key element of each unit. It is presented in an authentic context and ensures that students pay attention to accuracy, as well as become more proficient at expressing themselves clearly and precisely. The *Business communication* sections ensure that students are provided with a range of key expressions they can use immediately, both in the classroom and in their day-to-day work.

STUDENT'S BOOK

The *Student's Book* pack

The *Student's Book* pack offers a blend of classroom teaching and self-study, with an emphasis on flexibility and time-efficiency. Each of the 12 *Student's Book* units provides around five hours of classroom material with the potential for two to three hours of additional study using other materials in the pack.

The materials that support the *Student's Book* units are:

- *Viewpoint* video lessons
- Practice files
- Progress tests
- Photocopiable worksheets
- *Online practice*

More information on all of these materials and how to use them can be found later in these Introduction pages.

Key features of a unit

Starting point

Each unit opens with lead-in questions to raise awareness of, and interest in, the unit theme. Use these questions to find out what students already know about the topic and how it relates to their own working lives. These questions can be discussed as a class or in small groups.

Working with words

This section introduces key vocabulary in a variety of ways, including authentic reading texts. Students are encouraged to look at how different forms of words (e.g., verbs, adjectives and nouns) can be built from the same root, or look at common combinations (e.g. verb + noun, adjective + noun) that will help them to expand their personal lexicon more rapidly. This section also offers opportunities to work on your students' reading and listening skills.

Business communication

This section focuses on one of six broad communication themes – meetings, presenting, exchanging information, phone calls, negotiating and socializing. These are treated differently throughout the book so that, for example, students are able to practise exchanging information on the phone as well as face-to-face, or compare the different language needed for giving formal and informal presentations. Typically, the section begins with students listening to an example situation (a meeting, a presentation, a social encounter, a series of phone calls). They focus on *Key expressions* used by the speakers which are listed on the page. They are then given the opportunity to practise these in various controlled and more open work-related tasks.

Language at work

The grammar is looked at from a communicative point of view; this will meet your students' expectations with regard to learning form and meaning, but also reminds them how the grammar they need to learn commonly occurs in business and work situations. The target grammar structures are then practised in authentic work contexts.

Practically speaking

This section looks at various practical aspects of everyday communication and social interaction.

Key word

Commonly occurring words with multiple meanings are explored through short exercises in *Practically speaking*.

Culture question

One of the sections in each unit contains discussion questions which raise awareness of how national and company cultures can influence business interaction.

Talking point

The *Talking point* at the end of the unit provides the opportunity for students to discuss a range of business concepts, approaches and ideas and how they might apply these in their own work. All of the topics relate to the unit theme and provide another opportunity for students to use the language from the unit. The *Talking point* generally follows a three-part structure: Input (a short text, listening or infographic), Discussion, Task.

Viewpoint

At the end of every three units there is a two-page *Viewpoint* video lesson instead of a *Talking point*. The topic of the *Viewpoint* lesson relates to a theme from the preceding units and includes authentic interviews with leading business experts from Saïd Business School in the University of Oxford. Each lesson opens with a focus on the topic supported by discussion questions. Key words and phrases are then introduced before students watch the main video section, which includes a number of short videos on different aspects of the topic. Here, students can develop listening and note-taking skills with language presented in an authentic context. Each lesson ends with activities to give students speaking practice on the topics in the videos.

About Saïd Business School

Saïd Business School is part of the University of Oxford. It blends the best of new and old – it is a vibrant and innovative business school, yet deeply embedded in an 800-year-old world-class university. Saïd Business School creates programmes and ideas that have global impact – it educates people for successful business careers and, as a community, seeks to tackle world-scale problems. The school delivers cutting-edge programmes and ground-breaking research that transform individuals, organizations, business practice and society. Find out more at www.sbs.ox.ac.uk

Additional material

The following sections are in the back of the *Student's Book*.

Practice files

These provide unit-by-unit support for your classroom work. Each file provides additional practice of target language from *Working with words, Business communication* and *Language at work*. This can be used in two ways:

For extra practice in class – refer students to this section for more controlled practice of new vocabulary, grammar or key expressions before moving to the next stage. The optimum point at which to do this is indicated by cross references in the *Student's Book* unit and the teaching notes in this book.

For self-study – students can complete and self-check the exercises for review and revision outside class.

Answers for the *Practice file* exercises appear on pages 92–96 of this *Teacher's Book*.

Grammar reference

This provides grammar explanations relating to the *Language at work* section of each unit.

Useful phrases

This provides an extended list of phrases relating to the *Practically speaking* section of each unit.

Communication activities

Additional information for pairwork and group activities.

Audio scripts

TEACHER'S BOOK

What's in each unit?

Unit content

This provides an overview of the main aims and objectives of the unit.

Context

This section not only provides information on the teaching points covered in the unit, but also offers some background information on the main business theme of the unit, and its importance in the current business world. If you are less familiar with the world of business, you will find this section especially helpful to read before starting a unit.

Teaching notes and answers

Notes on managing the *Student's Book* exercises and various activities are given throughout, with suggested variations that you might like to try. You will find comprehensive answers to all *Student's Book* exercises, as well as notes on possible responses to discussion questions.

One-to-one

In general, you will find that *Business Result Second Edition* can be used with any size of class. However, with one-to-one students you will find that activities which have been designed with groups of students in mind will need some adaptation. The *Teacher's Book* provides suggestions for how to adapt group work activities successfully for one-to-one classes.

Pre-work learners

Although most users of *Business Result Second Edition* will be students who are already in work, you may also be teaching classes of students who have little or no experience of the business world. The *Teacher's Book* provides suggestions for how to adapt certain questions or tasks in the book to their needs, and extra notes are given for these types of learners.

Extension

With some students it may be appropriate to extend an exercise in some way or relate the language point more specifically to a particular group of students. Suggestions on how to do this are given where appropriate.

Extra activity

If you have time or would like to develop further areas of language competence, extra activities are suggested where they naturally follow the order of activities in the *Student's Book*. For example, if your students need writing practice or need to build more confidence with speaking, extra follow-up ideas may be provided for those aspects.

Alternative

With some students it may be preferable to approach an activity in a different way, depending on their level or their interests. These options are provided where appropriate.

Pronunciation

Tips on teaching pronunciation and helping students improve their intelligibility are provided where there is a logical need for them. These often appear where new vocabulary is taught, or where making key expressions sound more natural and fluent is important.

Dictionary skills

It's helpful to encourage students to use a good dictionary in class and the teaching notes suggest moments in the lesson when it may be useful to develop your students' skills in using dictionaries.

USING THE COURSE

How to use *Business Result Second Edition* to fit your teaching context

Business Result Second Edition provides all the flexibility you need as a teacher. The syllabus and content has been carefully designed so that it can be used either from start to finish, or in a modular way, allowing you to tailor the course to suit your and your students' needs.

Using the course from start to finish

You can, of course, use *Business Result Second Edition* conventionally, starting at *Unit 1* and working your way through each unit in turn. If you do so, you will find it works well. Each section of the unit is related thematically to the others, and there is a degree of recycling and a steady progression towards overall competence, culminating in the *Talking point* or *Viewpoint*. Timing will inevitably vary, but allow approximately five classroom hours for each unit. You will need more time if you intend to do the *Practice file* activities in class.

The 'flexible' option

Business Result Second Edition is written in a way that recognizes that many business English courses vary greatly in length. With this in mind, teachers can use *Business Result Second Edition* in a modular way. Although each unit has a logical progression, you will find that all the sections are essentially free-standing and can be used independently of the rest of the unit.

This modular approach provides the flexibility that business English teachers need when planning their course. Teachers might want to choose the sections or unit topics that are the most relevant and interesting to them and their students.

Online practice and teacher resources

For students

The *Online practice* gives your students additional language practice of the *Student's Book* content. For more information, see page 5 of the *Student's Book*.

For teachers

As well as providing access to all of the student online practice exercises, the Learning Management System (LMS) is an invaluable and time-saving tool for teachers.

You can monitor your students' progress and all of their results at the touch of a button. You can also print off and use student reports on their progress.

A training guide for how to use the LMS can be found in the *Guides* section of the *Online practice*.

Downloadable resources for teachers

The teacher resources in the *Online practice* include the following downloadable resources for teachers to use to complement the *Student's Book*:

- Photocopiable worksheets for every unit
- Progress tests for every unit
- Business cards for role-plays
- Class audio
- Class video

Photocopiable worksheets

New for *Business Result Second Edition* are the photocopiable worksheets. These provide extra communicative practice, often in the form of a game, for every *Working with words*, *Business communication* and *Language at work* section in the *Student's Book*.

There are suggestions in the *Teacher's Book* for when to use these worksheets in class. All of the worksheets, as well as the answer key, can be downloaded and photocopied from the teacher resources in the *Online practice*.

Photocopiable Progress tests

These can be administered at the end of each unit in order to assess your students' progress and allow you, the students, or the head of training to keep track of students' overall ability.

Each test is divided into two sections. The first section tests the vocabulary, grammar and key expressions from the unit. This section is scored out of 30 and students will need about 30 minutes to complete the questions.

The second section is a speaking test. In this section students are given a speaking task that resembles one of the speaking activities in the unit. These are mostly set up as pairwork activities in the form of role-plays, discussions or presentations.

Marking criteria is provided to help you assess students' performance in the speaking test. It requires students to perform five functions in the speaking test, and you can grade each of the five stages using a scoring system of 0, 1 or 2, giving a final score out of 10.

The speaking test role-plays can also be used as extra classroom practice without necessarily making use of the marking criteria.

All of the tests, and the answer keys, can be downloaded from the teacher resources in the *Online practice*.

Business cards

There is a set of downloadable business cards in the teacher resources in the *Online practice*.

The business cards are particularly useful to use in role-play situations from the *Student's Book* if you have students from the same company and they are required to exchange information about their company.

Class audio and video

All of the class audio and the videos for the *Viewpoint* lessons can be streamed or downloaded from the teacher resources in the *Online practice*. Students also have access to the class audio and video in their version of the *Online practice*.

Alternatively, class audio can be played from the audio CD and the videos can be played from the DVD that is found in the *Teacher's Book* pack.

How to access the *Online practice*

For students

Students should use the access card on the inside front cover of the *Student's Book*. This contains an access code to unlock the content in the *Online practice*.

For teachers

Teachers need to go to **www.oxfordlearn.com** and either register or sign in. If you are registered with the Oxford Teachers' Club, Oxford Learner's Bookshelf, or Oxford Learner's Dictionaries, you can use your existing username and password to sign in.

Then click on **Register an organization** and follow the instructions. Note that if you are not part of an organization, or you don't have an authorization code from your institution, you will need to click on **Apply for an organization account**. You will then be asked to supply some information. If you don't have an institution, then put your own name next to Institution name.

Teacher's website

Additional teacher resources can be found at **www.oup.com/elt/teacher/businessresult**

Unit content

By the end of this unit, students will be able to
- talk about cultural differences
- report on research and use tenses correctly
- introduce themselves.

Context

Building connections with other people and companies is integral to the success of any business, and in today's global business climate this often means building relationships with people and companies from different cultures. This is not always easy, since people from different cultures tend to interpret and evaluate situations in different ways. In order to develop successful business relationships across cultures, there needs to be appreciation of, and respect for, these cultural differences.

One of the key issues arising when cultures meet in a business context is the difference in value systems and how this has an impact on styles of decision-making. For example, people from individualistic ('I') cultures (e.g. the USA) tend to value personal goals and concerns over group goals and concerns, and personal rights over collective responsibilities. In contrast, people from collectivistic ('we') cultures (e.g. many countries in Africa and Asia) tend to value group goals and concerns over personal ones, and collective needs over personal needs. In a decision-making meeting, those from an individualistic culture might be more likely to behave competitively rather than cooperatively, and favour a decision that would maximize rewards or individual profit, whilst those from a collectivist culture are more likely to try to maintain group harmony and protect the interests of the whole group. If there is a lack of cultural awareness, these different approaches could cause misunderstandings or conflict.

In this unit, students have the opportunity to discuss different cross-cultural experiences. They then practise the language of participating in an informal meeting. They also review past, present and future tenses. To finish the unit on *Connections*, working across cultures and cross-cultural experiences, the *Talking point* is about working in multinational teams. Students then analyse issues that could arise, and come up with solutions.

Starting point

As a lead-in, write the words *cultural awareness* and *company culture* on the board. Ask students what they think these words mean and write their ideas on the board (e.g. *cultural awareness* = understanding and respecting the fact that people from different cultures have different values, customs, languages and traditions; *company culture* = accepted behaviour within a company, reflected in the organizational structure, work environment, dress code, values, working hours, overtime, etc.). Students then work in pairs and discuss the questions.

This can be a very sensitive topic. Throughout the unit, try to avoid generalizations and stereotyping.

Possible answers

1 Cultural awareness is needed if you are doing business with someone from another culture. Simple rules of etiquette are important so that you don't appear impolite. For example:
- In Japan, people greet each other by bowing.
- In France, you shouldn't use the familiar *tu* form, or use first names, unless invited to do so.
- In the USA, you might have a takeout lunch during a meeting. This is usually a sandwich you buy before the meeting and bring with you, and you might drink a coffee out of a plastic cup while walking to work. In Italy, you would be more likely to take a visitor for a longer lunch in a nice restaurant, and talk business over a coffee in a café. Americans are very conscious of time, whereas Italians place more importance on social rapport.
2 Company culture is influenced by styles of decision-making and by accepted styles of relationships between management and staff. The culture of the country where a company is based will determine what these accepted styles are.

PRE-WORK LEARNERS Write the following questions on the board and ask students to discuss them in pairs.

- *What cultural differences have you experienced when holidaying in other countries?*
- *What aspects of the culture in your country might be difficult for a foreign visitor to understand?*

Write the following numbers on the board and ask students if they have any significance in their culture.

13

888

4

Now write the following questions on the board and ask students to discuss their ideas in pairs.

1 *Which of these numbers is considered lucky in China? Why?*

2 *Which is considered unlucky in the UK? Why?*

3 *Which is considered unlucky in Japan? Why?*

Answers
1 888 – eight represents prosperity and joy in China
2 13 – the reason is not known for sure, but it could be linked to Christian tradition (the disciple who betrayed Jesus was the thirteenth to sit at the table at the Last Supper)
3 4 – in Japan the word for four is similar to the word for death

Working with words

Exercise 1

Students read the statements and decide if they agree with them. They can then discuss their answers in pairs.

Possible answers
1 No. Every company has its own way of doing things.
2 Not necessarily more weight, but body language/gestures communicate meaning; people also judge others according to how they are dressed, etc.
3 No. Some cultures are very time-conscious – being on time is very important; in other cultures it's less important.
4 No. Within every culture individuals vary enormously.
5 Yes. It's important to be open and accept that there are situations you won't necessarily understand.
6 Yes. It helps you to understand different styles and approaches to business and enables you to avoid offending business contacts from other cultures.

Exercise 2

Students read the text and compare their answers in **1**. Before they read, check that students understand *prerequisite* (something that is required as a prior condition for something else to happen or exist). Then with a partner they decide which piece of advice they find most useful. Ask students to justify their choice.

Possible answers
1 Each organization has its own culture, personality and way of doing things.
2 Noticing how people act, dress and treat each other can be helpful.
3 Cultures may have totally different concepts of time.
4 Values and behaviour are also influenced by background, experience and personality.
5 It's important, but this can be difficult. Business is about managing unknowns.
6 It gives you a better insight into working across cultures.

If your students lack knowledge about different cultures, ask them to do some research online for homework. Ask them to choose one country that interests them and to prepare a short talk for the next lesson giving advice about working with people from that country and/or visiting that country.

Exercise 3

Students complete the phrases with verb + noun collocations from the text. Remind students that we use *work **for** a company* when we are actually employed by that company. We use *work **with** a company* when we have dealings with another company, or we are self-employed and work at their site for a limited period.

Before students attempt **3**, ask them to see how many phrases they can complete without referring back to the text. Then give them just 30 seconds to find the answers in the text.

Answers

1	build	**7**	form
2	keep	**8**	manage
3	process	**9**	work
4	read	**10**	build
5	take	**11**	weigh up
6	keep	**12**	give

Exercise 4

Students now match the collocations from **3** to the definitions.

Answers

a	5	**g**	11
b	2	**h**	7
c	6	**i**	10
d	1	**j**	3
e	4	**k**	12
f	9	**l**	8

Exercise 5

Students work in small groups. If possible, put students from the same nationality or company together. Encourage them to use the collocations from **3** during their discussion.

Exercise 6

▶ **1.1** Students listen and answer the question.

Answers
Speaker 1: negative
Speaker 2: positive
Speaker 3: positive

Exercise 7

▶ **1.1** Students decide what each adjective is used to describe. They then listen again and compare their answers.

Answers
1 P **2** PL **3** E **4** E **5** PL* **6** P **7** P **8** E **9** P
10 P **11** E **12** E
* *up-and-coming* can also be used to describe a person who is likely to become successful or famous in the future.

Exercise 8

Students work in pairs. They match the definitions to six adjectives from **7** and then write their own definitions for the other six.

Answers
a 4 **b** 7 **c** 8 **d** 9 **e** 11 **f** 10
open-minded = willing to listen to, think about or accept different ideas
out-of-the-way = far from towns or cities, isolated, not central
time-consuming = taking or needing a lot of time
up-and-coming = likely to be successful and popular in the future
self-assured = having a lot of confidence in yourself and your abilities
unexpected = something you hadn't imagined would happen, a surprise

---

EXTRA ACTIVITY

Ask students to work in pairs and brainstorm the opposites to the adjectives in **7**.

Possible answers
1	narrow-minded	7	reserved
2	central	8	exciting
3	quick/rapid	9	head-in-the-clouds
4	interesting	10	difficult/demanding
5	past-it	11	high-profile
6	timid/shy	12	expected

Exercise 9

Students work in pairs and describe their experiences using the adjectives from **7**.

PRE-WORK LEARNERS Write the following questions on the board and ask students to answer them in pairs, using adjectives from **7**.

1 *How are you viewed at your college?*
2 *What is your college like?*
3 *Have you ever had a part-time job, or a work placement? If so, what was the experience like?*

Further practice
If students need more practice, go to *Practice file 1* on page 102 of the *Student's Book*.

Exercise 10

Allow time for students to think about one of the situations. They should then talk about their experiences with a partner, answering questions 1–4. Encourage them to use vocabulary from **3** and **7**.

Monitor for use of the new vocabulary. At the end of the activity, ask students to summarize their partner's situation. Give feedback on the use of vocabulary and correct mistakes if necessary.

PRE-WORK LEARNERS Write the following situations on the board and ask students to think about them.

- *You have shown visitors round your college.*
- *You have several new classmates joining an existing class.*
- *You studied in another country/college.*
- *You started a new course with people you didn't know.*

Photocopiable worksheet
Download and photocopy *Unit 1 Working with words worksheet* from the teacher resources in the *Online practice*.

Business communication

Exercise 1

Ask students to read the *Context*. They can then discuss the question in pairs.

Possible answer
Johanna will probably be expecting to hear details about the location, the facilities available, any competition in the area, property prices, etc.

EXTRA ACTIVITY

Write the following questions on the board. Ask students to work in pairs and discuss the answers (answers are in brackets).

What is the capital city of Poland? (Warsaw)
What is the population of Poland? (38.5 million)
What is the name of the sea to the north of Poland? (the Baltic Sea)
In which part of the country is the mountain location of Zakopane? (the south)

Students might also be interested to know that the main industries in Poland are electronics, vehicles and construction.

Exercise 2

▶ **1.2** Students listen and complete Johanna's notes.

Answers
1 Probable location = the Krakow area
2 General impression = up-and-coming place
3 Pros = beautiful, lively, a lot going on (personal observation)
4 the area is being invested in for development
5 Cons = a number of hotels already catering for the business market
Conclusions / action points
6 Several interesting sites worth considering outside Krakow
7 Action = go exploring, visit other sites

Exercise 3

▶ **1.2** Students listen again, put the points in **2** in the correct column, then note down the expressions, and decide whether the information comes from a personal observation or a third party/another source. They can then work with a partner and discuss why these expressions are used. You may have to pause the listening at various points to allow students enough time to note down the expressions.

Answers

1 What Peter has seen: 3, 5
  What someone else has told Peter/Johanna: 1, 2, 4, 6, 7
2 Expressions and their use in context:
1 Johanna says: '… because Krakow is such an up-and-coming place, they've told us that they definitely want the site to be somewhere in that area.' (Johanna may want to emphasize this is not her decision.)
2 Johanna says: '… because Krakow is such an up-and-coming place …' (This is the client's opinion.)
3 Peter says: 'Krakow is a fantastic place … which I have to say is absolutely beautiful and buzzing with life.' (Peter's view of Krakow which seems to echo that of the client.)
4 Peter says: 'According to the local tourist office, they're really investing in developing the area …' (This is what Peter was told, but it may not be 100% accurate.)
5 Peter says: '… however, from what I could see, there are already a number of hotels catering for the business market.' (In his short time of looking around the city, Peter felt there was already competition.)
6 Peter says: 'But I gathered from the locals I met, that there could be several interesting sites worth considering in the mountains outside the city.' (The locals told Peter there were other sites of interest around the city.)
7 Peter says: 'But they wrote the names down for me and I cut my stay in Krakow short and headed for the hills …' (Peter had been told to look at other alternatives and find out more.)

Exercise 4

▶ **1.3–1.4** Students listen to Parts 2 and 3 from the meeting and complete the table. You may have to pause the listening at various points to allow students enough time to note down the answers.

Answers

	1 Mountain site	**2** City outskirts site
Pros	breathtaking scenery, lots of activities going on	infrastructure is already in place; first class facilities, old brewery building available
Cons	more of a ski resort than a business centre; not close to the airport	cost of refurbishment of brewery site
Concerns	possible problems with people not speaking English well enough – communication problems	they haven't talked through the figures, Johanna's not convinced they will be acceptable to the client

Exercise 5

▶ **1.5** Students listen to the extracts from Parts 2 and 3 and note the expressions. They check their answers with a partner.

Answers

1 d 2 a, c 3 b

Exercise 6

Students work in pairs and read their information. Allow them five minutes to prepare to report their findings. Remind students to refer to the *Key expressions*. When they are ready, they should report back to each other. They can then discuss the differences in their information. While monitoring the task, check students are using the *Key expressions* correctly.

ALTERNATIVE Students could select a town or area that they know well to talk about. They could look for more precise information on the Internet.

Further practice

If students need more practice, go to *Practice file 1* on page 102 of the *Student's Book*.

Exercise 7

Students work in pairs. Allow time for them to prepare what they will say. They can then take turns to report back to each other. You could note any errors or particularly good uses of the language and then have a feedback session, putting the examples on the board. Students decide which sentences on the board contain mistakes and then correct them.

PRE-WORK LEARNERS Ask students to think of a project they have worked on or to pick a topic they are working on. Ask them to report back to the team on:

- how far on they are in the project
- what they have learnt about the topic
- any issues they have had to complete the project
- when they will complete the project

Exercise 8

Students discuss whether the language they used when reporting back in **7** gave the intended impression (e.g. positive or negative) to their partner.

Give positive feedback to students who used the *Key expressions* correctly.

Photocopiable worksheet

Download and photocopy *Unit 1 Business communication worksheet* from the teacher resources in the *Online practice*.

Language at work

Exercise 1

Students read sentences 1–7 and match them to meanings a–g.

Answers

1 e* 2 c 3 d 4 b 5 a 6 g 7 f
* In this example, what was decided in the past didn't happen, but this structure can also be used to describe a past plan that *did* actually happen at a later time.

Ask students to work in pairs and identify the tenses/structures that are used in the italic sections of the sentences in **1**.

Answers
1 past perfect
2 modal *should*
3 *be going to*
4 present perfect
5 present continuous
6 past perfect continuous
7 future continuous

Exercise 2

Students work in pairs and compare the pairs of sentences a–g.

Answers
a *has been telling* implies recent completed action/actions, focusing on the activity, not the result; suggests that this is a repeated action.
has told implies recent completed action, focusing on the present result; suggests they only told them once.
b There is only a slight difference in meaning. *have really been pushing* implies recent completed action focusing on the activity, not the result.
're really pushing implies very current activity, taking place around the time of speaking; the emphasis is on the fact that it is happening now and there is no mention of the past.
c *was looking around* implies an action happening around a main action in the past simple; sounds more like the beginning of a story.
had been looking around implies an action in progress before something else happened over a period of time in the past.
d There is very little difference in meaning here. Both sentences refer to a plan that was made in the past. *planned* refers to an action in the past and could be the main action.
had planned implies an action that happened before another action referred to in the past simple (the main action). It could also imply that the plan didn't happen depending on intonation and what follows.
e *should have gone* implies a lost opportunity; it refers to something in the past that you didn't do, but that would have been advisable to do and you regret not doing it.
should go is a simple recommendation.
f *could be* implies there's a possibility that it will be complicated.
's going to be implies certainty that it will be complicated.
g *'ll have written* talks about an action completed by a given time in the future.
'll be writing talks about an action in progress (but not completed) at a particular time in the future.

ALTERNATIVE Ask students to identify the tenses/structures in sentences a–g before they start the exercise.

Answers
a present perfect continuous, present perfect simple
b present perfect continuous, present continuous
c past continuous, past perfect continuous
d past simple, past perfect simple
e modal + *have* + past participle
f modal + verb, *be going to* + verb
g future perfect, future continuous

Grammar reference

If students need more information, go to *Grammar reference* on page 126 of the *Student's Book*.

Exercise 3

Students read the email and correct any tense mistakes. They should then look for verbs where a different tense could be used. They can then check their answers in pairs.

Answers
Mistakes:
~~had been skimming~~ have been skimming
~~was gathering~~ have gathered
~~should have pointed out~~ should point out
~~are being expected~~ are expected
~~had heard~~ have heard
~~we try~~ we have been trying / we tried
~~have been insisting~~ have insisted
~~I'll have got back to you~~ I'll get back to you
~~I know what will be happening~~ I'll know what is happening
Alternative verb forms:
It won't be (isn't going to be) as straightforward as we had hoped. – tone doesn't change
If we haven't heard (don't hear) by then. – tone doesn't change
We need (will need) to take legal action. – tone doesn't change
We need to take (we will be taking) legal action. – tone changes: the alternative sounds like a definite plan, so is more formal/decisive

Further practice

If students need more practice, go to *Practice file 1* on page 103 of the *Student's Book*.

Exercise 4

Students work in pairs and find out as much information as they can about each other. Encourage them to use a variety of tenses in their conversations.

Note down any incorrect uses of tenses during the activity. Afterwards, write the errors on the board for the whole class to correct.

PRE-WORK LEARNERS Tell students that it's the first day at their new place of study and they're trying to get to know each other during a break. Write the following topics on the board and ask students to talk about them with a partner.

- *a major change (perhaps you've moved town to study at the place you are now)*
- *how you ended up choosing the course you're on*
- *any present projects (perhaps you've joined a club/ sports team)*
- *your regrets and hopes*
- *your predictions*

Photocopiable worksheet

Download and photocopy *Unit 1 Language at work worksheet* from the teacher resources in the *Online practice*.

Practically speaking

Exercise 1

As a lead-in, write the following statement on the board and ask students if they agree with it. Then ask them to work in pairs and discuss the questions.

First impressions are always right.

Exercise 2

▶ **1.6** Students listen and answer the questions.

Possible answers

Answers will vary, but students might make some of the following observations:

Speaker 1 hasn't structured her presentation very well, although her warning that she can talk too fast might be appreciated.

Speaker 2: She's much more formal, but could be seen as a bit arrogant because she gives herself lots of credit (although she does want to share her knowledge, which is positive).

Speaker 3: This is very informal (some might see this as good, others will see it as bad) and he is also quite boastful.

Speakers 2 and 3 show cultural differences also in how they use language and how they describe themselves.

Exercise 3

Students order the information and compare their answers in pairs.

Answers

1 who they are
2 role
3 reason for being there
4 achievements/activities
5 aspirations

Exercise 4

▶ **1.6** Students listen again and complete the phrases. They can then work with a partner and match the phrases to the topics in **3**.

Answers

1 my name's, I'm from
2 I'm accountable for
3 I've now managed to
4 Lately I've been concentrating on
5 I'm ready to
6 those of you who don't know me already, I am
7 My responsibilities include
8 I'm empowered to, have the task of
9 I'd like to point out that, I have been continually improving
10 I hope to
11 As most of you will know
12 Basically, my role is to
13 this entails a lot of
aspirations: 10
role: 2, 7, 8, 12, 13
who they are: 1, 6, 11
reason for being there: 5, 10
achievements/activities: 3, 4, 9

Useful phrases

Refer students to the *Useful phrases* section on page 134 of the *Student's Book* for extension and revision.

Exercise 5

Allow time for students to prepare their introductions. Encourage them to choose phrases from **4** to use in their introduction. Then ask each student to introduce himself/ herself to the class.

Give feedback on the use of language in the introductions and the impression each student made on the rest of the class.

ALTERNATIVE If you have access to the necessary equipment, you could film the introductions. Ask students to prepare their introductions for the next lesson. You can then film and play back the footage to the class. Ask students to watch themselves and their classmates and comment on the following:

Language
- expressions used (particularly new ones from the unit)
- accuracy of tense use
- range of vocabulary

Delivery
- pace
- pronunciation of key words
- body language (gestures, eye contact)

KEY WORD

Students match the phrases to the definitions.

Answers

1 b   2 e   3 a   4 d   5 c

CULTURE QUESTION

Students can discuss the questions in pairs, before comparing answers with the rest of the class.

Progress test

Download and photocopy *Unit 1 Progress test and Speaking test* from the teacher resources in the *Online practice*.

Talking point

Discussion

Exercise 1

Tell students to read the article and ask them what the writer states are the main reasons for problems arising in multinational teams. Be prepared to answer any questions about vocabulary, for example, *exacerbate* (v) = to make something worse, particularly a problem or illness. It is generally used in formal English.

Students can discuss the question in pairs, before comparing answers with the rest of the class. Ask students to give examples of their experiences where possible.

Possible answers

Answers about experiences will vary.

The writer claims the main problems experienced in multinational teams are misunderstandings brought about by differences in culture and expectations.

Exercise 2

Ask students to read the emails and final response. Ask students to discuss with a partner what Jack and Namrata are thinking in each response and what they expect to happen.

Answers

Email 1 – very direct request, almost sounds like an order; no use of expected polite phrases like *please / thank you*. Jack expects Namrata to send the necessary information immediately. Namrata is probably unpleasantly surprised to get an email which sounds so abrupt.

Email 2 – personal questions may not be appropriate; however, this is not uncommon in some cultures where building a rapport with colleagues is important. Paragraph 2 is irrelevant, the request is delegated and therefore delayed. Jack might be annoyed that this is being passed on to someone else.

Email 3 – too direct again. Jack sounds either very stressed or very annoyed. The impatient tone is very clear.

Email 4 – very vague about information; more irrelevant information as far as Jack is concerned.

Email 5 – very direct, sounds rude to many cultures, for example, the UK, because there are no greetings or goodbyes or *please / thank you*. Jack will not get the response he wants.

Email 6 – Namrata is now extremely angry and will probably do as little as possible to help Jack. His tone has probably offended her.

Exercise 3

Ask students to look at the emails and improve them so that they sound efficient and polite. You could ask them to rewrite Jack's emails and swap them with another pair who write Namrata's responses. Ask the group to decide which emails would be most successful.

Possible answer

Possible solutions might be discussing what they find most helpful in emails. The aim is for Jack to get the information he needs without offending Namrata, and for Namrata to sound efficient, and perhaps give less irrelevant information. Perhaps they could have an informal discussion over coffee about the differences they've found between cultures and what's surprised them about working in a multinational situation. This might sensitize them to each other's problems.

Task

Exercise 1

Students work with a partner and go through the list of complaints, analysing what the problem is and coming up with a solution for each.

Divide students into small groups and ask them to give the solution his/her pairing came to. They can also give reasons for their choices.

You could ask students to decide the best solution to each problem in these groups, and give the reasons for their choice. For whole-class feedback, each group reports its best solution and the class picks the best solution to each problem.

Possible answers

Problems:

Employee shows lack of confidence, is unable to show any initiative.

Work-related social life intruding on employee's personal life.

If everything is factual, it is impossible to gauge how people feel about the situation/decisions, etc.

Employee feels underappreciated. The system for promotions is not clear.

Employee's workload is too much? It is certainly not planned, therefore employee does not have clear objectives. This is demotivating as they never know when they've achieved what is expected.

Boss/colleague cannot accept disagreement due to lack of confidence or perhaps arrogance.

Solutions:

Students' own answers

Exercise 2

Students stay in their groups and discuss their own experiences.

EXTRA ACTIVITY

Ask students to write an email detailing one of the problems. Ask them to explain what solution the group chose and give reasons for the choice.

ONE-TO-ONE Your student and you go through the questions in the *Discussion* together. In the *Task*, your student should read the complaints, analyse the problem and come up with a solution. He/she can then talk about their own experiences.

2 Careers

Unit content

By the end of this unit, students will be able to

- talk about careers
- discuss/share ideas and talk about the past
- explain their opinion.

Context

Today, most of us need to adopt a more flexible and proactive attitude towards our careers. The notion of a 'job for life' in the same company is no longer valid, even in countries like Japan, where companies have traditionally been more paternalistic towards their staff. Competition for jobs is no longer confined to individual companies or countries: globalization of the economy means that employees are competing for jobs with people in low-cost countries like India and China. Employees at all levels, from the senior manager to the most unqualified production worker, have to be aware of how they can move up in their companies and what additional skills they will need to acquire if they still want to be employable in five or ten years' time.

Companies, too, realize that a key element in the recruitment and retention of employees is the opportunities they offer them for career development. They can no longer promise them the job security of twenty years ago. However, they can at least provide them with the knowledge and experience they need; either to continue to be of value to the company, or to pursue their careers elsewhere, if necessary.

In this unit, students talk about the best ways of moving up in a company and the different career development possibilities on offer. They practise the language of managing discussions and sharing and clarifying ideas. They also review past modals and third conditional sentences for expressing attitudes to the past. In the *Talking point*, they discuss the 'gig' economy and how it will change the future of careers. They will then discuss how they could develop skills in a 'gig' situation.

Starting point

Students can discuss these questions in pairs before comparing answers with the rest of the class. You could monitor and make a note of any incorrect (or correct) past modal forms or conditionals to go over when you get to *Language at work*. You may find the second question is rather sensitive if students aren't happy with their present job. Don't force them to answer this if that is the case.

PRE-WORK LEARNERS Ask students to talk about their study choices with a partner instead of career choices. If they have experience of work placements or internships, they could talk about these.

Working with words

Exercise 1

Check students understand what *patchwork* is. Draw their attention to the picture of the traditional patchwork quilt to help them get the idea. Check students understand what *working freelance* means. Then ask students to think what being a *patchworker* might be. For example, ask them what the difference between working as a *freelancer* and a *patchworker* is. Then brainstorm possible areas where people could *patchwork* in their occupation.

PRE-WORK LEARNERS Write *freelancer* on the board. Ask students to work with a partner and make a list of the pros and cons of working as a freelancer. Then ask them to look at Cardinale's definition and say in what ways working as a patchworker is different.

Possible answers

The *patchworker* is essentially a sole trader who sets up their own business, but is actually more concerned with having a good work/life balance. This gives them flexibility about when they work. The company has the work done, but does not have to pay the normal costs of a permanent employee – tax, health insurance, holiday pay, etc., nor does it have to guarantee work. The advantage of patchworking is that you can fit it around your lifestyle. It gives opportunities for freelance workers to engage in many different aspects of a project, to multitask. It also allows them to demonstrate their creativity, while enjoying the feeling of being in control of their career. It gives freedom to make decisions. It can be very hard, challenging work, but is actually very rewarding.

Exercise 2

Before students read the text, read out the questions only and ask students to write them down. Ask students to discuss why they think Cardinale came up with these questions to help you decide if you could be a patchworker. Ask them for one or two suggestions for the answers. Students then read the text and compare their suggestions with Cardinale's. You could ask them how they feel about patchworking. Ask them if they think they have what it takes to be a patchworker.

Exercise 3

Students work in pairs to decide on definitions for the multi-word verbs. Before they start, you might like to elicit one definition from the class as an example. They think of definitions for the other multi-word verbs in bold in the extract in **2**, using the context in the text to help.

Possible answers
1 to produce an answer, solution, idea
2 to become extremely tired or sick by working too hard over a period of time
3 to be noticeable; to be recognized as different or better
4 to push yourself in front of the competition
5 to resist somebody; to not accept bad treatment from somebody without complaining
6 to make sure you have an advantage
7 to act in the role of
8 to make sure that you stay friendly with somebody, because you will get an advantage from doing so
9 to be prepared to go and do something (which may be difficult)
10 to support or defend a person or idea

DICTIONARY SKILLS

Ask students to work in pairs and choose four of the multi-word verbs in **3**. Give them three minutes to find the verbs in a dictionary and identify which example sentences in the dictionary entry match the meaning used in the texts. The winners are the first students to find all four.

Exercise 4

Students work in pairs and choose the six multi-word verbs in **3** that they find most useful. They should then write questions to ask a partner. If they find it difficult to make questions only about careers, extend the subject to anything work-related. They then take turns with their partner to ask and answer each other's questions.

Possible answers
1 Can you come up with any ideas for making your job more interesting?
2 What sort of things in your job/studies could you feel burnt out from? / Have you ever felt burnt out from your job?
3 What would you do to stand out from competitors? / Which of your company's products stands out from the rest?
4 What strategies do you have to motivate yourself and propel your career forward?
5 Do you find it easy to stand up to people in authority? / Have you ever had to stand up to your boss?
6 How do successful companies stay ahead of their competitors?
7 Have you ever had to play the part of one of your managers? / What problems could you have playing different parts when patchworking?
8 What sort of things could you do to keep in with useful contacts? / How important is it for staff in your company to keep in with their boss?
9 Would you feel comfortable getting out there and selling yourself? / If you're looking to grow your business, what should you get out there and do?
10 Is it easy to stand up for what you believe in at work?

Exercise 5

▶ **2.1** Before students listen to the interview, ask them what they think a *career coach* is (someone who helps you in planning and managing your career). Ask the class who should be more responsible for career development – the employee or their company. Encourage an exchange of views, then refer students to the questions. Students can check their answers in pairs before comparing answers with the rest of the class. During feedback, ask students if they agree with the views expressed.

Answers
1 false
2 true
3 false

Exercise 6

▶ **2.1** Students match the verbs to the phrases. They can then listen again to check their answers.

Answers
1 h 2 f 3 e 4 c 5 a 6 g 7 b 8 d

ALTERNATIVE Dictate or write on the board the sentences from the listening in **6** in random order with the verbs and phrases gapped (answers are in brackets). Ask students to complete the sentences, making any changes to the verbs that are necessary.

1 *If you want to (move forward), you need to take responsibility for your own career development.*
2 *Ask around for advice and see what you can do about (following less conventional paths).*
3 *Something else to remember is that, over time, you will (grow into your role).*
4 *There are times when we (reach a stage) in our careers when we feel stuck.*
5 *Being assigned to other departments or project teams ... needn't mean you're being side-lined – your (horizons) are simply being (broadened).*
6 *You want to (go beyond the scope of) your current job, ... so you start looking around for an interesting position in another organization.*
7 *Sometimes, in order to move forward you need to (take a step backwards) to (put yourself in a better position) for the next move.*

Exercise 7

Students work with a partner and match the phrases to the definitions. During feedback, ask students for any examples they can give based on their own experience.

Answers
a 1 b 2 c 8 d 5 e 4 f 3 g 6 h 7

Further practice

If students need more practice, go to *Practice file 2* on page 104 of the *Student's Book*.

Exercise 8

Students work in pairs. They should work together to prepare an outline for their talk. Ask them to think about where they could incorporate vocabulary from **3** and **6** in their talk. Students then take turns to listen to their partner giving the talk. They can then give feedback to their partner on the language he/she used. If you have time, you might like to ask some students to give their talk to the whole class. For whole-class feedback, monitor and note any correct/incorrect use of the phrases from **3** and **6**. After the activity, write the sentences that contain these phrases on the board and ask students to identify the correct sentences and amend the incorrect sentences.

PRE-WORK LEARNERS Ask students to work in pairs and prepare a talk for the next lesson. Tell them that the talk is for recent university graduates and the title is as follows:

Building a career – what companies can offer you.

For homework, students could research the subject on the Internet, searching under the key words *career development*.

Photocopiable worksheet

Download and photocopy *Unit 2 Working with words worksheet* from the teacher resources in the *Online practice*.

Business communication

Exercise 1

Ask students to read the *Context* before asking them to think about what issues may be discussed during the meeting. You could also ask them if their companies have similar problems with recruitment.

Possible answers

What would the training needs of school-leavers be?
How would suitable school-leavers be selected?
What would the conditions of employment for school-leavers be?
Will school-leavers have to work the same number of hours with the same salaries as graduate trainees?
Will taking on school-leavers have an impact on the quality of work completed by the company and therefore affect the company's reputation?
Would graduates be better for the company?

Exercise 2

▶ **2.2** Students listen to extract 1 of the meeting and make notes on 1–3.

It is probably a good idea to give feedback on questions 1 and 2 first and then play the listening again to allow students to focus on the expressions used. Ask if they can think of any other expressions that might be used to invite someone to contribute, e.g. *Could you / Would you like to / Would you mind … go(ing) over … / tell(ing) us about / fill(ing) us in on …*

You may need to check students understand the meaning of *digression* (talking about something that is not connected with the main point of what you are saying, or moving away from the main point).

Answers

1 Both issues in the first point are covered.
2 just after each of Arun's contributions to the discussion
3 start meeting: *… so let's get started, shall we?*
establish meeting objectives: *The purpose of today's meeting is to …*
ask Arun to present his findings: *Perhaps Arun, you'd like to talk us through some of your findings.*
get Arun to talk about this: *Arun, did you want to talk about staff retention issues as well?*

Exercise 3

▶ **2.3** Students listen to extract 2 of the meeting and discuss the answers in pairs, before comparing answers with the rest of the class. You could then ask them what they think of the idea and if a similar policy exists or would be useful in their company (or country).

Answers

1 An in-house training / apprenticeship programme would be set up for them, whereby they would work and study at the same time. They would be paid modestly for the five-year duration of the plan.
2 A lot of good students are worried about the cost of being at university and being in debt. They would be happy to have secure employment.
3 Rachel thinks school-leavers are too young to make career decisions, and therefore might not be as committed to the profession as a graduate.

Exercise 4

Students match the expressions to the categories individually before comparing answers with the rest of the class.

Answers

a 2 **b** 1 **c** 4 **d** 3

Exercise 5

▶ **2.2–2.3** Play the listening twice without stopping. Ask students to note down at least one phrase for each category in **4**. Then ask students to compare their answers and add any expressions they missed.

Answers

1 The obvious solution to this problem must be to …
I know you're not keen on it, but …
I'm sure you'll understand the need to …
I'm not sure what your feelings are about this, but …
We were wondering if …
Given that … wouldn't it be better to …?
Something else we've been thinking about is …
2 I'm sorry, but …
What makes you so sure …?
But surely …?
… it's interesting you should say that, because actually …
I suppose so.
But do you really think …?
3 If I could just come in here for a moment …
Would this be the right moment to mention …?
4 Go ahead.
I'll get on to that in a moment.
Coming back to the issue of …

Exercise 6

Elicit answers from the whole class.

Answers
1 I know you're not keen on it, but …
  You probably won't like this idea, but …
  I'm not sure what your feelings are about this, but …
2 We were wondering if …
  Something else we've been thinking about is …
3 I'm sure you'll understand the need to …
  The obvious solution to this problem must be …

Further practice

If students need more practice, go to *Practice file 2* on page 104 of the *Student's Book*.

Exercise 7

Allow time for students to read through the list, then elicit any other ideas they might have.

Possible answers
Select the graduate recruitment fairs carefully and make sure the benefits of the graduate scheme are clear.
Increase starting salaries for the departments where there is most difficulty recruiting.
Perhaps introduce an increment scheme for graduates who complete specific training rather than introducing penalties.
Select a graduate employee to edit the blogs, etc. on the company website.
Hold open days at the company site for graduates to come and look round, ask questions, etc.

Exercise 8

Students work in pairs and have the meeting. Encourage students to use language from the *Key expressions* and follow the flow chart. Students can then change roles and have the meeting again.

For whole-class feedback, monitor and note any correct/ incorrect use of the language from the *Key expressions*. After the activity, write the sentences that contain these expressions on the board and ask students to identify the correct sentences and amend the incorrect sentences.

Exercise 9

Students work in groups of three. Ask each group to choose a chairperson (Student A). Allow a few minutes for Students B and C to read their information, Student B on page 137 and Student C on page 139, and come up with any new ideas. During this time, ask Student A to note down any ideas he/she can think of for each point on the agenda. Students then have the meeting. Encourage them to use language from the *Key expressions* where appropriate. Students should reach a decision on each item of the agenda.

When the activity has finished, ask Students B and C to evaluate how well Student A managed the meeting and involved both speakers. Ask Student A to evaluate how respectful Students B and C were of others' opinions, i.e. did they interrupt each other too much or did they criticize ideas too directly? You could ask them how easy they found it to interrupt, and how they felt being interrupted.

EXTENSION Ask students to write up the minutes of the meeting for homework. They can use the agenda to help them structure the minutes. Ask them to include:

- at least two ideas that were rejected for each agenda item
- reasons why those ideas were rejected
- one or two ideas that were accepted for each agenda item
- reasons why those ideas were accepted

ONE-TO-ONE Ask the student to read the Student B information on page 137. He/she can then chair the meeting, making Student B's points. You are Student C. Make sure the learner manages the discussion and brings the meeting to a close.

CULTURE QUESTION
Students can discuss the questions in pairs before comparing answers with the rest of the class. The following ideas may arise, but be careful to avoid over-generalizing.

- Generally, in Asian cultures it is considered impolite to disagree with a hierarchical superior.
- In Northern European cultures diplomacy and politeness are often used to disguise real disagreement.
- In Latin cultures passionate disagreement is fairly common.

Photocopiable worksheet

Download and photocopy *Unit 2 Business communication worksheet* from the teacher resources in the *Online practice*.

Language at work

Exercise 1

▶ 2.4 As a lead-in, write on the board one thing about the past you are happy about, and one thing you regret.
For example:

1 *I passed my driving test first time.*
2 *I refused a teaching job in Australia.*

Elicit how you could express satisfaction about 1 and regrets about 2. Make a note of students' suggestions on the board and ask them to correct any mistakes.

Before they listen to the debriefing conversations, ask students if they can remember what the initial meeting in *Business communication* was about. If they haven't worked on *Business communication*, briefly establish the context for the listening: four people in an accountancy firm have just had a meeting to discuss the HR department's idea to recruit school-leavers and are saying what they thought of the meeting. Students then listen and complete the sentences.

You might want to check that students understand *it's just as well*. Explain that it's similar to *it's lucky*.

Answers

1 I'm so glad I finally had
2 it's just as well I brought you along
3 I'd thought about it, I could have brought
4 It would have been good if we'd made
5 if only I'd known
6 we should have anticipated
7 might have been
8 could have been awful if
9 suppose I hadn't been there to present
10 would have happened if I hadn't suggested
11 still don't think Arun brought
12 it's a good thing he came

Exercise 2

Students can compare their answers in pairs before comparing with the rest of the class.

You might want to check that students understand the following:

relieved = feeling happy because something unpleasant has not happened or is over.

hindsight = the understanding that you have of a situation only after it has happened and means that you would have done things in a different way.

Answers

a 1, 12
b 2, 8, 9, 10
c 5*, 11
d 3, 4, 5*, 6, 7
* could be c or d

PRONUNCIATION Ask students to look at the sentences in **1** again. Write the following tasks on the board (answers are in brackets).

- *Underline any contracted forms.* (*I'm, I'd* x 2, *we'd* x 2, *hadn't* x 2, *don't, who's, it's*)
- *What other contractions could be used in these sentences?* (*could've* x 2, *would've* x 2, *should've, might've*)

Then drill the pronunciation of these new contractions and ask students to practise them in pairs. Ask them when it is more suitable to use contracted forms (in spoken language, in less formal situations) and when it is preferable to use full forms (in written language, in more formal situations).

Exercise 3

Students match the sentences in **1** to the structures. If students are unfamiliar with the grammatical terms, ask them to give you examples from the sentences of a conditional sentence, a modal, a past simple, and a past perfect form.

Answers

a 3, 4, 10
b 6, 7, 8
c 1, 2, 11, 12
d 5, 9

Grammar reference

If students need more information, go to *Grammar reference* on page 126 of the *Student's Book*.

Exercise 4

Check that students understand how the 'nearly CV' works by asking them to tell you what actually happened, e.g. *When he (or she) graduated from university, he looked for a job to get some experience and was offered a job abroad.* Then focus on the first situation (1a) and elicit sentences using the target structures, e.g. *Maybe he should have studied for a postgraduate degree. But if he'd studied for a postgraduate degree, he might not have got useful work experience abroad.* Students then work in pairs. Monitor and ask students to self-correct if you hear any mistakes in the target structures. Give feedback on possible answers with the whole class.

Further practice

If students need more practice, go to *Practice file 2* on page 105 of the *Student's Book*.

Exercise 5

Ask students to think about choices they made in their career in the past and the options they rejected. Give an example, such as a school you decided to study or teach at and another job you refused. If necessary, they could also think about study or job choices, or even towns they decided (not) to live in or houses/flats they decided (not) to buy. Students then discuss their past choices in pairs. Monitor and note down three correct sentences you hear and one incorrect sentence.

After the activity, dictate these four sentences at normal native speaker speed, using contracted forms where appropriate. Students write down the sentences and identify which one is incorrect.

PRE-WORK LEARNERS Instead of their work experience, students can focus on schools, academic subjects, sports or other hobbies they chose or didn't choose, good or bad teachers they had or were lucky/unlucky not to have.

Photocopiable worksheet

Download and photocopy *Unit 2 Language at work worksheet* from the teacher resources in the *Online practice*.

Practically speaking

Exercise 1

Refer students to the picture and the question.

> **Possible answers**
>
> You can use language to:
> - ask if someone has understood
> - give the listener an opportunity to ask for clarification
> - repeat what you said in a different way – perhaps using more simple vocabulary
> - give an example of what you mean
>
> You could also use your voice or body to:
> - change your intonation
> - make gestures
> - refer to visual aids

Exercise 2

▶ **2.5** Students listen and complete the sentences. You might need to play the listening twice to allow students to note down all the phrases. Students can then check their answers in pairs before comparing answers with the rest of the class.

> **Answers**
> 1 would it help if I gave you an example
> 2 I was actually referring to
> 3 if you look at, you'll see
> 4 sorry, let me rephrase that
> 5 What I'm saying is that
> 6 In other words
> 7 the fact of the matter is
> 8 the point I'm trying to make is
> 9 what I mean by 'well-informed' is
> 10 to put it another way

Exercise 3

Students match the phrases in **2** to the techniques.

> **Answers**
> a 4, 6, 10
> b 2, 5, 8, 9
> c 1, 3
> d 7

Exercise 4

Students work in pairs. Refer them to the agenda, then ask them to read their information on pages 137 and 139 of the *Student's Book*. Students then have the meeting. Monitor and ask students to self-correct where necessary.

> **Useful phrases**
> Refer students to the *Useful phrases* section on page 134 of the *Student's Book* for extension and revision.

Exercise 5

Students work in pairs and take turns to ask and answer questions. Encourage them to use the phrases from **2**.

PRE-WORK LEARNERS   Ask students to work in pairs. They take turns to ask each other questions on the topics in the list below. Ask for clarification on any details which aren't clear. Respond using the phrases from **2**.

- Your progress in class this year/term
- Your current assignments and research and how you are organizing your workload
- How you deal with stressful situations, for example, giving presentations, taking exams

> **KEY WORD**
> Students match the sentences to the uses of *so*. They can then check their answers in pairs before comparing answers with the rest of the class.
>
> **Answers**
> 1 d   2 a   3 c   4 b

Progress test

Download and photocopy *Unit 2 Progress test* and *Speaking test* from the teacher resources in the *Online practice*.

Talking point

Discussion

Exercise 1

Before students read the article, write *gig economy* on the board and ask them to discuss what they think it is and if they can think of one advantage to working in a 'gig' economy. You could ask them if they have heard of a gig in any other context (usually musical, as mentioned in the text). You can remind them of the text on patchworking and how 'gigging' and 'patchworking' could be connected. For example, you can choose when you work and so can have a better work-life balance.

You might want to check that students understand the following:

naysayer = a person who opposes or expresses doubts about something

portend = to be a sign or warning of something that is going to happen in the future; especially something bad or unpleasant

dystopian = relating to an imaginary place or state in which everything is extremely bad or unpleasant

disenfranchised = when someone has their rights taken away

hybrid = the product of mixing two or more different things

Students read the article and discuss whether their ideas are the same as the writer's.

> **Answers**
> A 'gig' economy is a system where people decide to work for short periods which suit their lifestyle, taken from the idea of a musical 'gig'.

Exercise 2

Ask students to decide what sort of jobs they think would work best in the 'gig' economy and write a list.

Ask them to compare the jobs they wrote in their list as suitable for a 'gig' economy with the ones the writer mentioned.

> **Answers**
>
> Jobs mentioned in the article: driver (Uber); (artisan) retailer (Etsy); (part-time) hotelier (Airbnb). The company TaskRabbit is also mentioned which relates to doing various odd jobs.

Exercise 3

Students work with a partner and complete the list of pros and cons of a 'gig' career. They can start with their own ideas and then add any others mentioned in the article.

> **Possible answers**
>
> Pros: flexibility of working hours; freedom to work as you want to; being your own boss
> Cons: workers have few rights; they have to chase after each piece of work; no company-provided benefits

Exercise 4

Each student gives his/her own answer to the question, and his/her reasons for the choice. You could ask students if they or any of their friends have any experience of working this way.

Exercise 5

Ask students to work in small groups and come up with two or three risks. They then discuss the risks in whole-class feedback.

> **Possible answers**
>
> Difficult to plan, and take on long-term financial commitments (like a mortgage, school fees, etc.) when you are not working permanently or full-time.
> Companies have to rely on there being the right people available at the right time for their work schedules.

Task

Exercise 1

Allow each student time to read the quote and decide what they would like to do. Ask them to think about how they can persuade others that their idea is feasible. Tell them to look at the chart in **2** and be ready to answer questions in each section.

You can find more information about Arun Sundararajan by searching online.

PRE-WORK LEARNERS Ask students to work in small groups. Each group comes up with a list of skills that they think could be useful to work in the 'gig' economy, for example, driving, experience in working in retail or tourism in holiday jobs, creative talents like baking cakes, cooking, woodwork, etc. Then ask them to think of something they would like to do as a 'gig on the side' while studying. They can complete the chart in **2** to help them prepare for the meeting.

When they divide into groups for the meeting in **2**, make sure you mix the groups so one person from the original group can explain their ideas to the new group.

Exercise 2

Divide the class into small groups. Students then have the meeting where each student presents his/her ideas in turn and the others in the group use the chart to ask questions. Ask them to aim to achieve total clarity in the exchange of ideas and equal involvement of all the participants.

You could ask each group to decide which of the 'gigs' they heard about would be the most successful. Ask them to give reasons for their choice.

When each group has finished, ask students to comment on their own performance.

Write the following questions on the board to help them:

- *Did you cover all points on the chart?*
- *Were the ideas/proposals clear to all participants?*
- *Were all participants equally involved in the discussion?*

EXTENSION As a follow-up activity, ask students to send an email to you, summarizing what was discussed. Give feedback on the language used. Deal with any corrections in the next lesson. You could also encourage students to correct each other's emails if you prefer.

ONE-TO-ONE The student can read the article. You can then do the *Discussion* questions together. In the *Task*, you can hold the meeting where the student tries to persuade you his/her idea is feasible.

3 Change

Unit content

By the end of this unit, students will be able to

- talk about organizational change
- give a formal presentation about the future
- show understanding.

Context

The topic of *Change* is extremely relevant in today's business world. Individuals now fully expect to change jobs several times during their careers. The days of working nine to five in the same company and climbing the career ladder have ended. Companies have always had to embrace change in order to achieve success, and continue to do so to maintain profits. However, they are now increasingly finding that they have to change working practices in line with technological innovations and increasing concerns about the environment. Implementing change can be a complex process due to the fact that there is often a natural tendency to want to avoid change. Companies have to manage any changes extremely carefully if they want to avoid negative reactions from their staff. Communicating exactly what will happen, why and when is part of ensuring that staff still feel in control and are more willing to accept change.

In the first section of this unit, students will talk about where they work and how working practices in their company may have changed over time. In *Business communication* they practise how to give a formal presentation. They then move on to look at the different future tenses needed to speculate about future change. In the *Viewpoint* video students watch two interviews. The subject discussed in the interviews is how organizations implement change and the impact change has on the individuals within organizations.

Starting point

As a lead-in, you could bring in some photographs of some famous buildings, e.g. the Gherkin in London, the Sydney Opera House, the Reichstag in Berlin, the Burj al Arab in Dubai. Alternatively, you could ask students to name some famous buildings they know. Then write the following questions on the board:

- *Why are these buildings so famous?*
- *What do you think of the internal/external design of these buildings?*

Discuss these questions as a class. Students can then work in pairs and discuss questions 1–3 before comparing answers with the rest of the class. Write any new vocabulary on the board.

You may have students whose work situations may not be secure. If that is the case, you may like to miss out question 3.

Possible answers

1 Students' own answers
2 Flexible working could include working part-time, flexitime, job sharing, working from home, working on short-term contracts, etc.
3 Answers will vary. Students may mention changes to working times and hours or technology used at work, changes in contract, etc.

PRE-WORK LEARNERS   For the first question, ask students to think about the building where they are studying or living. For the third question, ask them to discuss how they think the style and conditions of work are different now from when their parents started work.

Working with words

Exercise 1

Students read the text and discuss the question in pairs. Before they read, you might want to check that students understand *to have an aversion to* (to have a strong feeling of not liking something/somebody).

ALTERNATIVE / PRE-WORK LEARNERS   Ask students to work in small groups. Write the following instructions on the board:

- *Read the statements in the article.*
- *Using ideas in the statements and your own ideas, create a list of criteria for the ideal working organization.*
- *Present your ideas to the rest of the class.*

Exercise 2

Students compare their answers to the statements in the article in **1** and discuss any differences.

Exercise 3

Students look back at the article in **1** and find words in bold that are similar in meaning to those in italics.

Answers

1	effective	6	putting in place
2	access	7	procedure
3	means	8	purpose
4	option	9	dynamic
5	transformed	10	implement

Exercise 4

Students now decide if the words they found in the text could replace the words in italics in **3**. They should then decide if the meaning of the sentence would change. Ask them to discuss their answers with a partner. They can refer to dictionaries to help them if necessary.

Answers

1 Both words could be used, but the meaning would be slightly different. *Efficient* means that somebody or something that is able to do something well or successfully without wasting time, while *effective* means that something works well and the result is good.
2 Only *enter* could be used here as the sentence refers to a period of time. *To enter* means to go into a place or begin a period of time, while *to access* means to be able to get into something, e.g. a file or a place.
3 Both words could be used, but the meaning would be quite different. *Ability* means having the skill to do something, while *means* are having the resources you need to do something.
4 Both words could be used, but the meaning would be slightly different. *Opportunity* means the chance to do something, while *option* means choice.
5 Both words could be used, but *transformed* sounds much more dramatic than *changed*. *To change* means to make some alterations which may or may not be visible, while *to transform* means to change completely in a way that is clearly visible.
6 Only *carry out* is possible as a collocation of *research*. *To carry out* means to do something, while *put in place* means to set up something.
7 Only *process* is possible here. *Process* refers to a series of actions completed in order to achieve something, while *procedure* refers to the way or system of doing something.
8 Both words could be used, but the meaning would be different. *Meaning* means the significance of something, while *purpose* means the reason for something.
9 Both words could be used, but there would be a slight difference in meaning. *Energetic* means showing a lot of enthusiasm and determination, while *dynamic* means being full of energy and new ideas.
10 Only *install* is possible as a collocation of *software*. *To install* means to put in, while *to implement* means to put in place.

Exercise 5

▶ **3.1** Before students listen, write the words *consultancy* and *consultant* on the board. Ask students to brainstorm the activities that they associate with them (e.g. give advice, increase efficiency, oversee change, maximize profitability, facilitate projects). Then tell students BICG stands for Business Intelligence Consulting Group. Students then listen and answer questions 1–3.

Answers

1 infrastructure, i.e. information and communication technologies; the physical environment, i.e. architecture and use of office space; cultural aspects, i.e. working practices
2 It helps companies move with the times; implement cost-saving measures; become more productive; have more efficient and effective processes, teams and working practices; raise the level of motivation.
3 People at the bottom of the hierarchy tend to be quite happy to get something new; those at the top of companies are the champions or sponsors of these new concepts so will naturally be happy about them. However, middle management tend to be very resistant to change.

Exercise 6

▶ **3.1** Students listen again and note down the nouns.

Answers

1 needs/requirements
2 results
3 problems
4 cultural change
5 enthusiasm
6 information / knowledge / ideas
7 progress
8 success

Exercise 7

Students work in pairs and match the verbs in **6** to the nouns.

Answers

a 2 **b** 1 **c** 5 **d** 6 **e** 8 **f** 4 **g** 7 **h** 3

Exercise 8

Students work in pairs and make sentences to say how they could make their organization more efficient. Encourage them to use collocations from **6** and **7**.

Possible answers

I'm not sure that my company places importance on *accommodating the needs* of its employees. For example, we can't work flexitime. This isn't good for me because I've got children and I can't organize my day so that it fits in with school hours.
In my company, the managers *assess performance* by having appraisals every four months. In those meetings we are given performance objectives that we have to meet within a certain period of time.

PRE-WORK LEARNERS Write the following topics on the board. Ask students to work in pairs and make sentences using collocations from **6** and **7** (possible answers are in brackets).

- *A teacher you know* (Our teacher *generates enthusiasm* in the class by making the activities interactive.)
- *Your place of study* (*Progress is assessed* by testing every term.)
- *Your ideal working situation* (The company could *facilitate my development* by providing training.)

Further practice

If students need more practice, go to *Practice file 3* on page 106 of the *Student's Book*.

Exercise 9

Students work in pairs and read the email. They then have the meeting, following steps 1–3.

> **Possible answers**
> 1 The main points from the email: low productivity is a result of lack of motivation and low morale in the factory workforce. This results in workers doing the minimum, supervisors applying pressure to increase productivity and workers feeling under-appreciated.
> 2, 3 Ideas could include: ensuring that all staff have received adequate training to use new technology in production; introducing flexitime and ensuring that shift times accommodate the needs of employees; introducing bonuses for employees who exceed their targets, etc.

For whole-class feedback, monitor, making notes of any errors you want to discuss with the whole class. Give positive feedback to students who use verb/noun collocations from this section.

> **EXTRA ACTIVITY**
> Ask students to write a report based on the meeting for homework. Ask them to include the following:
>
> • an outline of the main problems
> • possible solutions discussed in the meeting
> • the agreed action plan

Photocopiable worksheet

Download and photocopy *Unit 3 Working with words worksheet* from the teacher resources in the *Online practice*.

Business communication

Exercise 1

Students work with a partner and discuss the questions.

Exercise 2

▶ 3.2–3.5 Students read the *Context*. They then listen and fill in the notes on the slides. Allow them to write notes for each extract before moving on to the next extract.

> **Possible answers**
> 1 Research from Henley Management College: middle managers are under increasing pressure and it's going to get tougher.
> 2 *demuting* = working remotely from wherever you are
> 20th century = 47.6-hour week for British workers
> 21st century = new generation of 'career nomads'
> 3 Employees will be working harder and longer unless organizations devise formal policies to deal with new working practices.
> *shadow careers* = amateur activities are pursued to professional standards
> Local communities could be revived if more people work from home.
> 4 Employers will have to tempt people away from working for themselves, rather than from working for the competition. Employers need to recognize the choice available to the workforce and start planning for it now.

Exercise 3

▶ 3.2–3.5 Students listen to the four extracts again and note down the expressions used for each function. They can then check their answers with a partner.

Exercise 4

Students turn to audio scripts 3.2–3.5 on page 147 of the *Student's Book* to check their answers.

> **Answers**
> 1 … just to fill you in on some of the background …
> 2 … I'll return to this point later.
> 3 I've divided my talk up into three sections. First of all, I'll …, After that, I'll …, and I'll conclude with …
> 4 I'd like to start by saying a few words about …
> 5 By *demuting* I mean …, Now, I don't know if you're familiar with this term? Well, … refers to …
> 6 OK, moving on now to look at …
> 7 … this is where …, and perhaps here I should just explain what I mean by … – that's when …, So, for example …
> 8 Turning to the next point, …
> 9 … and as I said earlier, …
> 10 Just to digress for a second …
> 11 And this brings me to the last point.
> 12 So, that brings me to the end of my talk. Thank you very much for listening. And I'll be happy to take any questions now.

Further practice

If students need more practice, go to *Practice file 3* on page 107 of the *Student's Book*.

Exercise 5

Students work in pairs and prepare a presentation summarizing what they found out from the listening in **2** and using the expressions from **3**. They then decide who will deliver each section and practise giving the presentation to each other. Monitor, giving help where necessary.

Ask students to give their presentations to the rest of the class. Give feedback on their style and use of language.

Exercise 6

Students prepare their presentations individually. You might need to help them come up with an idea for change, e.g. no more business trips, introduce flexible working, make all offices open-plan, allow employees' input on salary scales, allow employees to evaluate their bosses.

Refer them to the *Key expressions* list during preparation and remind them that the tone should be formal.

ALTERNATIVE Ask students to prepare the presentation for homework. They can then research the topic further and prepare slides/visuals.

ONE-TO-ONE Ask the student to think of a change he/she would like to make in his/her company and prepare a presentation on a proposal including the points in **6**. Refer the student to the *Key expressions* and signposting the structure of a presentation and remind him/her to keep the tone formal.
The student then gives the presentation. You listen and ask two or three questions to make sure the student has to refer backwards / forwards / sideways and explain or give examples to make sure you understand the proposal.

PRE-WORK LEARNERS Write the following ideas for a change at their place of study on the board. Students then choose their favourite idea and prepare to give a formal presentation outlining the change.

- *no more lectures/classes before 11.00 a.m.*
- *limit class sizes to 15*
- *introduce online teleconference-style lectures*
- *allow students to design the curriculum*

Exercise 7

Students work in groups and listen to each other's presentations. Encourage them to make notes so that they can check they understand and ask questions after each.

You could dictate the following categories for them to give peer feedback in their groups after the talks. The categories could include:

- a well-structured presentation with clear signposting and good use of the expressions and language in the *Key expressions* and to describe the proposal
- accurate use of language, grammar, vocabulary and pronunciation
- the right tone/level of formality
- other features important for a successful presentation, for example, good eye contact, clear confident voice, good pace, etc.
- whether the questions he/she asked were relevant

> **CULTURE QUESTION**
> Discuss the questions as a class. You could ask students to pick a country and find out from the Internet what their attitude to humour in a business situation is.

Photocopiable worksheet

Download and photocopy *Unit 3 Business communication worksheet* from the teacher resources in the *Online practice*.

Language at work

Exercise 1

Students can work in pairs to answer questions a–d about each of the sentences 1–10.

Answers

1 a future simple *will*
  b very
  c *be going to* + infinitive
  d the use of *be going to* would suggest that the speaker thinks there is more evidence in support of the prediction
2 a future perfect continuous
  b fairly, but the use of *estimated* in the sentence reminds us that it's a prediction
  c The future perfect simple could be used.
  d The future perfect continuous emphasizes the action of working will have started previously and will still be going on at that time in the future, whereas using the future perfect simple would mean that the action may have finished at this point.
3 a future continuous
  b fairly
  c *will* or *be going to* + infinitive
  d no significant change in meaning, but the use of the future continuous emphasizes the activity of working and raises the level of formality slightly
4 a *be going to* + infinitive
  b very
  c *will*
  d The use of *be going to* rather than *will* suggests that the speaker has evidence to support their argument.
5 a modal verb + infinitive
  b not certain, but there is a possibility
  c could be replaced by *be going to have, will have* and other modals could be used, e.g. *might / may / would*
  d It would alter the degree of certainty. *could/may* means that the speaker thinks it's slightly more likely to happen than if they used *might*, and using *would / will have / be going to have* would mean that the speaker is more certain that there will be 'other positive side effects'.
6 a future simple
  b fairly
  c As it is a prediction, *be going to* is possible.
  d *be going to* implies that the speaker has evidence to support their views
7 a *to be* (present simple) + adverb + infinitive
  b fairly
  c several, e.g. *will probably, be going to, be bound to*
  d Some structures change the meaning, i.e. *be bound to* means you think it is extremely certain.
8 a future perfect simple
  b fairly
  c could be replaced by future continuous, e.g. *will be taking place*, or with another modal verb, e.g. *may/might*
  d Using the future continuous would mean that the change will be in progress in the middle of the 21st century, but using the future perfect simple means that the change will have already occurred by this point. Using different modals would affect the levels of certainty
9 a present simple passive + *be* + *-ing* form
  b very
  c no, but word order could change, e.g. *It is expected that people will be working …*
  d no change in meaning
10 a modal + adverb + infinitive
   b very
   c *will / be going to*
   d no change in meaning

Write the following phrases on the board. Focus on the weak verb forms of *have* and *been*. Ask students to practise saying the weak forms.

- *will have been working* /wɪləvbɪnwɜːkɪn/
- *will have taken place* /wɪləvteɪkənpleɪs/

Grammar reference

If students need more information, go to *Grammar reference* on page 127 of the *Student's Book*.

Exercise 2

▶ **3.6** Before they listen, ask students if they think there will be a major change in the way we work in the future. Write the phrases they use to make their predictions on the board. Then students listen and note down the phrases used. They can then compare their answers with the phrases on the board.

Answers

1 … it's bound to happen sooner or later.
2 It may happen, but it's not very likely.
3 I think it's possible that we'll see new innovations in this area, yes.
4 It may well be that things change in the next few years.
5 Definitely, yes – there's certain to be a major change at some point in the future.
6 I think it's very unlikely that will happen, to be honest.
7 Oh, most certainly, yes. And it's highly likely to impact on all our lives.
8 It's quite probable that we'll see some big changes in the near future.
9 It's certain that there will be significant changes, yes.
10 Oh, definitely, and there's a good chance most of us will benefit from these changes.

Exercise 3

Students categorize the phrases. They can then check their answers in pairs before comparing answers with the rest of the class.

Answers

a certain: it's bound to, definitely, there's certain to be, it's certain that, most certainly
b probable: it's highly likely to, it's quite probable that we'll, there's a good chance
c possible: it may happen, it's possible that we'll, it may well be that
d unlikely: it's not very likely, it's very unlikely

Elicit phrases for the future that could be used if you think something is impossible (e.g. *we definitely won't …, we've got no hope of -ing …, there's no chance we will …, there's no way we will …*).

Exercise 4

▶ **3.6** Students listen again and note the phrases referring to a point/period of time in the future.

Answers

sooner or later
in the next few years
at some point in the future
in the near future

Further practice

If students need more practice, go to *Practice file 3* on page 107 of the *Student's Book*.

Exercise 5

Allow students time to note down some ideas before telling their partner about their predictions. Remind them to use a variety of phrases to express certainty and uncertainty about the future.

Write the following topics on the board. Ask students to choose a topic and make predictions about it.

- *The economy in your country*
- *Standards of living in your country*
- *The environment*
- *Your future career*
- *Your future living arrangements*

Photocopiable worksheet

Download and photocopy *Unit 3 Language at work worksheet* from the teacher resources in the *Online practice*.

Practically speaking

Exercise 1

▶ **3.7** As a lead-in, write the following work-related problems on the board.

- *My office is too noisy.*
- *I don't like giving presentations.*
- *I have too much work to do.*
- *I'm so disorganized.*

Ask students how they would show understanding if a colleague spoke to them about these problems. Write any suggested language and/or techniques on the board.

Then ask them to listen and identify the problems and the listeners' responses.

Pre-teaching vocabulary will give the answers to **1**, so just tell students you will deal with any unknown words after the listening. You might then want to check that students understand the following:

to be snowed under = to be very busy

treading water = not moving forward

to badger someone = to repeatedly ask someone for something

Answers

speaker 1 The first speaker has a lot of work, and the other speaker responds by empathizing and explaining that they are in a similar situation.
speaker 2 The second speaker's presentation didn't go according to plan. The other speaker agrees that the organization at the conference hasn't been great, and makes a suggestion.
speaker 3 The first speaker feels that they are spending most of the time passing on messages now that the team has split up, and cannot get on with work. The other speaker empathizes.
speaker 4 The first speaker is annoyed because nobody has responded to a message. The other speaker makes a suggestion.

Exercise 2

▶ **3.7** Students listen again and complete the phrases. They can then compare their answers with a partner before comparing with the rest of the class.

Answers
1 what you mean
2 hectic over here too
3 hasn't, has it
4 might be worth
5 what you're saying
6 know this is a tricky time
7 see where you're coming from
8 had a similar problem
9 still think you should send
10 you might want to

Exercise 3

Students match the phrases in **2** to categories a–c.

Answers
a 1, 3, 5, 7
b 2, 6, 8
c 4, 9, 10

EXTRA ACTIVITY

Ask students to work with a partner and think of other phrases they might use for a–c in **3**. Write their suggestions on the board.

Possible answers
a I get your point. / Quite. / Absolutely. / Exactly. / I know.
b I see what you mean. / We're going through the same thing here.
c Why don't you …? / Maybe you could try …? / What if you were to …?

Exercise 4

Students discuss possible responses to sentences 1–4.

Possible answers
1 I know what you mean. (It's quite hectic over here too).
2 I had a similar problem when I gave a presentation last week.
3 I know what you mean. I thought it was very confusing too.
4 I see where you're coming from – you might want to have a chat with Paul about it.

Useful phrases

Refer students to the *Useful phrases* section on page 134 of the *Student's Book* for extension and revision.

Exercise 5

Students work with a partner and think of a problem at work or choose one from the list. They take turns to explain the problem and respond.

Students discuss their partners' reactions with the class. For whole-class feedback, focus on the correct use of phrases for showing understanding and on correct intonation. Check that students sound genuinely sympathetic.

KEY WORD

Students match the sentences to the synonyms for *quite*.

Answers
1 c 2 a 3 b 4 e 5 d

Progress test

Download and photocopy *Unit 3 Progress test* and *Speaking test* from the teacher resources in the *Online practice*.

Viewpoint 1

Preview

The topic of *Viewpoint 1* is *Dealing with change*. The video lesson examines how organizations implement change and the impact change has on individuals. Students watch two different interviews with Louise Fitzgerald, Visiting Professor of Organizational Behaviour, and Jonathan Trevor, Associate Professor of Management Practice, who both lecture at the Saïd Business School, which is part of the University of Oxford.

You could ask students if they know anything about the Saïd Business School. For information on the Saïd Business School check the website, https://www.sbs.ox.ac.uk.

Allow time for students to read the *Preview*.

Exercise 1

Tell students they are going to watch two interviews on the topic of change. The interviewees are university lecturers at the Saïd Business School. Tell students they will hear the speakers using the 12 sets of words and phrases in the video. Students match the words and phrases to the definitions a–l. They then compare answers with a partner.

Answers
1 g 2 e 3 i 4 l 5 k 6 j 7 h 8 f 9 a 10 b
11 d 12 c

Exercise 2

Students work with a partner. They choose six of the words in **1** to write six gapped sentences, as in the example.

Exercise 3

Student pairs work with another pair, taking turns to read the sentences saying 'gap' for the missing word. The other pair then guesses the missing word to win a point. The pair that scores the most points wins. If there are words neither pair have chosen, then ask the group to come up with a sentence for each of those.

Exercise 4

▶ 01 Ask students to read the *Profile*. To get them thinking about the topic, you could ask them what problems can occur when there is organizational change, for example, employees feeling nervous about the possibility of redundancy, lack of engagement/interest in new ideas, resistance to new systems, etc.

Students then watch Professor Louise Fitzgerald talking about dealing with organizational change and the three key aspects to consider. Students number A–C in the order she talks about them.

Answers
A 3 B 1 C 2

Exercise 5

▶ 01 Before students watch the video again, ask them to read the questions carefully and make a few notes on what they can remember from the video. They watch the video again and complete their notes. They can then discuss their answers with a partner.

Answers
1 It should be based and founded on a robust analysis of what's happening currently in the organization.
2 Analysis should be cross-checked to get a wider perspective, so hard data plus what managers and senior staff think, but also what junior staff and customers think about what's happening.
3 An organization should engage its staff in the process.
4 Staff need to have some understanding of what's going on and be engaged in various ways – for example, to offer perspectives that haven't been understood before, and to help the process along.
5 That change takes time.

Exercise 6

▶ 02 Students watch the second part of the interview where Louise Fitzgerald gives more detail about how to implement change. Tell students to match each item in the list to each of the key aspects of organizational change in **4**, labelling them A, B or C. They check their answers with a partner.

Answers
Trend data B
Benchmarking B
Surveys B
Human resource management data B
Managers and working groups (project teams) C
Interviewing staff during the disruption C
Reappraisal and review A

Exercise 7

▶ 02 Students watch the second part of the interview again and write down further details about each item in **6**. They compare and discuss their answers in small groups and add any missing details.

> **Answers**
> Trend data: shows how things are going over time.
> Benchmarking: what's happening in your organization compared with what's happening in other organizations in the same sector.
> Surveys: attitudinal data, e.g. attitude surveys, customer satisfaction feedback, are useful because it gives some element of foundation for trying to pre-judge how people will respond to the change.
> Human resource management data: helps company understand what is happening in the company.
> Managers and working groups (project teams): useful if they are cross-sectional, people with different backgrounds, from different departments, they know the detail so you can work out how the plan will be delivered.
> Interviewing staff during the disruption: ask them if there is anything you could do alongside the change so the organization can get maximum benefit out of the disruption.
> Reappraisal and review: need to be planned at regular intervals to include staff, so they can give feedback on the process. The company can then make changes if necessary.

Exercise 8

In small groups, students think of an organizational change they have been involved in and describe the points on the list to the group. They can then report back their ideas to the class. Encourage students to use the words and phrases in **1** and the language from the interview.

Then give positive feedback on the use of language and write any mistakes on the board for the class to correct.

EXTENSION Ask students to appoint a spokesperson from each group who can present the further details on each item to the whole class.

PRE-WORK LEARNERS Ask students to think of a change they have been involved in at their college/university and describe it to the group.

Exercise 9

▶ 03 Draw students' attention to the *Glossary*. Ask them to give an example sentence for each of the words. Before students watch the video, ask them to discuss with a partner how they might feel if their organization was going through a big change. Ask students to read the *Profile*. Then ask them to read the changes a–g. They watch and tick the changes that Jonathan Trevor mentions.

> **Answers**
> a, c, e, f

Exercise 10

▶ 04 Students watch Jonathan Trevor talking about some of the issues in **9**. They make notes about 'losers' and 'winners' in the table. Then they compare and discuss their answers with a partner.

> **Answers**
> **Losers (negative impact)**
> Perhaps more 'losers' than winners, there is fear and uncertainty about the future of work
> Middle class wages not rising (across the developed world)
> **Winners (positive impact)**
> Companies in the knowledge economy
> Entrepreneur types/those who have opportunities to take advantage of the changes of structure

Exercise 11

Students work in groups. Ask them to look back at the list of changes (a–g) in **9** (including those not mentioned by Jonathan Trevor), and to discuss them in relation to the questions. Make sure they give reasons for their answers.

Exercise 12

Students think of a major change that has had a positive or negative impact on organizations and the individual worker in the last 20 years and tell the class about it. If students find it hard to come up with anything, you could ask them to research changes on the Internet and then present what they found out to the class. You could suggest areas like company organization, developing new markets, technology, and how these have changed in a particular company.

ONE-TO-ONE Ask the student to discuss change in his/her organization, what the change was, why it was brought in, how it was organized, and what the involvement and reaction of the employees was.

Further ideas and video scripts

You can find a list of suggested ideas for how to use video in the class in the teacher resources in the *Online practice*. The video scripts are available to download from the Teaching Resources on the Oxford Teachers' Club. www.oup.com/elt/teacher/businessresult

Unit content

By the end of this unit, students will be able to

- discuss company risks
- participate in a teleconference and use pronouns to refer to something
- facilitate conversation.

Context

Life is full of risks for everyone. Getting out of the shower or doing DIY (Do It Yourself), like building bookshelves or repairing a tap, should be done with care; deciding whether to wear a helmet or not when riding a bike depends on your attitude to risk. In business, risk management has become a vital decision-making tool. Due to the fact that virtually every decision involves some element of uncertainty, and because there are risks inherent in most of the key issues facing companies today, the ability to understand risks and manage them effectively is an important ingredient for success. Risks are present whenever a company decides to expand into a new market, or to launch a new product. Similarly, companies are exposed to external risks, such as political or economic changes in the countries in which they operate, new technology and shifts in social behaviour.

In this unit, students learn about different kinds of risk and are encouraged to discuss the various risks facing their own company. They have the opportunity to practise the language of managing discussions, checking understanding, and expressing opinions in the context of teleconferencing. They also review the use of pronouns as reference markers. In the *Talking point* they examine and discuss the risks faced by organizers of large international sporting events and how these risks may be avoided.

Starting point

Refer students to the quotes and check they understand what they mean (Ray Bradbury quote = risk-takers just do something and deal with problems as they come up; David Lloyd George quote = to achieve something important you have to take risks). Before they start, you may want to check students understand *chasm* (a deep crack or opening in the ground, often used to describe a very big difference between two people or groups, for example, because they have different attitudes).

Students can discuss the questions with a partner before comparing answers with the whole class.

Working with words

EXTRA ACTIVITY

Elicit what kind of risks we have to evaluate and manage in our daily lives, e.g. whether to leave home without your cycling helmet because you're late for work and can't find it, and so run the risk of being injured if you're knocked off your bike.

Ask students to think about some areas of daily life in which we are sometimes encouraged to take risks, like sports, and which are the areas where taking risks is unacceptable.

Exercise 1

Discuss this question as a class and brainstorm risks faced by businesses. Write students' suggestions on the board.

Possible answers

Investment in new products – may or may not be a commercial success.
Investment in new technology – will probably be obsolete within a few years.
Moving into new markets – cultural sensitivities, different working practices, local laws.
Employing someone on the basis of one interview and their CV – they may not fit in.
Takeovers – could lead to staff issues and redundancies, differences in infrastructure and in shareholders' objectives, legal problems, etc.
Giving credit to new customers – they may not pay on time, leading to cash-flow problems.

Exercise 2

Students read the article individually, then discuss their answers in pairs. Compare answers as a class.

Before they read, you might want to check that students understand the following:

be immune to = not to be affected by something

be littered with = have many examples of something (used in a negative sense)

blatantly = in an open way without caring if people are shocked

Answers

1 They should have contingency and communications planning in place and run simulation tests of crises.
2 If they try too hard to avoid legal complications, it may lose them sympathy or support in the public eye.
3 the CEO
4 by the reaction of the company and how the crisis was handled, rather than what the crisis actually was

---

EXTRA ACTIVITY

Ask students to think of five nouns that collocate with *risk* (the title of the unit) (e.g. *management*, *assessment*, *factor(s)*, *analysis*, *manager*) and two adjectives that collocate with *risk* (e.g. *possible*, *unnecessary*, *potential*, *inherent*). You could ask them to check possible collocations in a dictionary.

You could ask them to look up synonyms for *risk*, for example, *danger*, *hazard* and *threat*, and find the adjectives, prepositions, etc. that collocate with them. Possible examples are:

in danger/out of danger, extreme/grave/great danger, face danger, reduce danger

major/potential/environmental/health hazard, pose a hazard to, deal with a hazard

considerable/serious/significant/imminent threat, pose a threat, see something as a threat

---

Exercise 3

Students match the phrases in bold in the text in **2** to the definitions 1–9. They can then check their answers in pairs.

Answers

1 run simulation exercises
2 expressing care for
3 be (surprisingly) resilient to crises
4 take ownership
5 show public remorse
6 have robust communications plans in place
7 restore (its) reputation
8 learn from (each) other's mistakes
9 start with (some proper) contingency planning

Exercise 4

Students work in pairs and discuss what advice they would give. Encourage them to use the phrases in **3**. You might like to ask them to tick off the different phrases as they use them or hear them used.

Exercise 5

▶ 4.1 Students listen and answer the questions. They can then discuss their ideas in pairs before comparing answers with the rest of the class.

Possible answers

Speaker 1: CEO, risks = signing agreements, cutting prices, managing shareholders' money
Speaker 2: Sales Representative, risks = what deal to offer, who to follow up – risk of time-wasting
Speaker 3: Actuary (Risk Assessor), risks = potential risks in a company – both health and safety and external risks

Exercise 6

▶ 4.1 Students listen again and note which speaker uses the adjectives.

Answers

Speaker 1: over-cautious, reckless, bold, rash, imprudent, prudent, foolhardy
Speaker 2: sensible, cautious
Speaker 3: prudent, risk-averse*
* Note that *risk-averse* is not generally used to describe decisions/actions.

Exercise 7

Students decide which adjectives in **6** have a positive and which have a negative connotation. Ask them to check their answers in pairs before comparing answers with the rest of the class. When checking answers, point out that *risk-averse* could have a positive or negative connotation depending on the context and the attitude of the speaker. If necessary, you could ask students to check in their dictionaries for exact definitions.

Answers

Positive connotation: sensible, cautious, prudent, bold
Negative connotation: imprudent, reckless, rash, foolhardy, over-cautious, risk-averse*
risk-averse is considered negative in the listening, but it could also be perceived as positive in other contexts

Exercise 8

This activity allows students to focus on the exact meanings of the adjectives in **6**. Students work in pairs. When checking their answers with the class, make sure that they can pronounce the words correctly. If necessary, ask them to mark the word stress on the adjectives of two syllables or more (see word stress marked in answers). They could practise these by working with a partner, giving definitions for the other students to guess the word and say correctly.

Suggested answers

1 risk-a<u>ver</u>se, (over-)<u>cau</u>tious
2 <u>sen</u>sible, <u>pru</u>dent
3 im<u>pru</u>dent
4 <u>reck</u>less, rash, <u>fool</u>hardy, bold

Exercise 9

Students work in pairs and discuss people they know. You might like to give an example to help them. Try to describe someone who has a very different attitude to risk from you. For example: *I've got a friend who constantly speculates on the stock market and invests in risky business ventures. He used his son's student loan to invest on the stock market – and made enough money for his son to cover his university costs. I'd never take that risk! He says he's prudent, because he studies the market carefully. I think he's very bold and maybe a bit foolhardy!*

When getting feedback from the rest of the class, avoid asking students to talk about their own attitude to risk as they might not want to share this with everyone.

Check that students are using the adjectives correctly, with appropriate positive or negative connotation.

Ask students to work in pairs or groups of three. Their task is to write a questionnaire to find out how risk-averse the class is. Each group should write two questions, with a, b or c answers. They can then join with another group to come up with four questions for their questionnaire. When they are ready, they can circulate and ask their questions. When they finish, they collate the answers with their original group and summarize their findings for the class, using adjectives from **6**.

You could write the following example on the board to start them off:

You're on a skiing holiday. You've skied three times before in your life. Your friend, who's a very good skier, wants to take you on a black run, saying it'll be fun. Do you:

a *accept without hesitation – you'll be safe with your friend and it'll be great?*

b *say you'll think about it – maybe tomorrow, when you've had a chance to look at the slope?*

c *say 'no way'?*

EXTENSION Ask students to imagine they are in a job interview. One of the questions is:

What risks are you exposed to at work and what is your attitude to them?

Give students ten minutes to prepare their answer, before presenting it to the class.

Ask students to work in small groups and ask each other the questions. In each group they decide who is the most risk-averse and who is willing to take big risks. Then the whole class compares their outcomes and decides who is the most willing to take big risks.

You may find students are more comfortable with doing feedback in their groups. If a student is more risk-averse, he/she might feel embarrassed to admit that in open-class feedback.

Further practice

If students need more practice, go to *Practice file 4* on page 108 of the *Student's Book*.

Exercise 10

Before students do the exercise, ask them to spend a few minutes deciding what they think a company's internal strengths, weaknesses and external opportunities and threats would be (a SWOT analysis). You could ask each group to think of a different type of company, for example, a car company like Volkswagen, or Toyota, a soft drinks company like Coca-Cola or Pepsi, or a retail chain like Zara or Marks & Spencer.

Students then work in pairs to carry out their PEST analysis. If possible, create pairs of students from the same company or from companies in a similar field of business. Explain that they should focus on the risks (or threats) to their business rather than the opportunities. Encourage them to use new words from this section where possible.

PRE-WORK LEARNERS Elicit the names of some companies students know (e.g. a supermarket, a clothing brand, a petrol company). They could be international or local companies. They can then prepare a PEST analysis for their chosen company.

Exercise 11

Ask each pair to present their findings. You may prefer to deal with each point on the PEST analysis separately, i.e. all the pairs report on the political factors first, then the economic factors, etc. This may invite further discussion on the similarities between the different sectors or companies.

Ask students to self-correct if you hear a target word being used incorrectly or the wrong word being used. Otherwise, let the discussion flow freely.

Photocopiable worksheet

Download and photocopy *Unit 4 Working with words worksheet* from the teacher resources in the *Online practice*.

Business communication

Exercise 1

Students work in pairs to think of advice for participating in a teleconference for the first time. When they have finished, ask the class if there is anything in the guidelines on page 138 of the *Student's Book* that they disagree with. If they take part in teleconferences themselves, ask which guidelines are most often not respected.

Exercise 2

▶ 4.2 As a lead-in to the listening, ask students what risks traditional travel agents are facing today, and what they are doing about them, e.g. developing their own online sites in response to 'virtual' travel agents; offering new solutions to those tired of traditional packages, such as 'pick and mix' holidays, adventure tours, accommodation in local people's houses; offering more holistic holidays; offering 'green' holidays for people concerned about the environmental cost of the travel industry.

Ask students to read the *Context*. Students read the agenda and then listen with the guidelines on page 138 of the *Student's Book* in front of them so that they can tick the guidelines that are followed. Compare answers with the whole class.

Before they listen, check that students understand the following:

pipe dream = a hope or plan that is impossible to achieve, or not practical

carbon offsetting = calculating your carbon emissions and purchasing 'credits' from emission reduction projects

Answers
1 Everyone seems to be familiar with the agenda.
2 Jean-Luc and Khalid talk over people.
3 Nobody introduces themselves each time they come into the conversation. Jean-Luc doesn't identify everyone. Thomas, Joana and Greta don't identify themselves, but they might have done before extract 1. Khalid identifies himself.
4 Jean-Luc nominates Greta to speak.
5 Thomas checks he's understood correctly.
6 Thomas digresses. Jean-Luc keeps people to the agenda and encourages everyone to do the same.

Exercise 3

Students work with a partner and categorize the expressions.

Answers

a 1, 7*, 12	**d** 4, 6, 15
b 5, 8, 10	**e** 3, 9, 14
c 2, 11, 13	

*Note that 7 could also fit category d.

Exercise 4

Discuss the differences between the two sets of expressions with the whole class. You could then ask which style is closer to meetings held in the students' own language.

Possible answers

A is more formal/tentative (*Could you …? / Am I right …? / I'd be interested … / Can I just …? / We seem …*) whilst B is much more direct/less formal.

Exercise 5

▶ **4.3** Students listen and decide what the speaker really means in each case. Stop the listening after each extract and elicit possible answers from the whole class.

Possible answers

2 You've said enough. Let Joana speak.	**4** That's enough!
3 I don't agree.	**5** This is irrelevant.

Exercise 6

Elicit an example from the whole class for the first item. Students then work in pairs to decide on possible answers.

Possible answers

1 X, could you talk us through this?
2 You're saying that …
3 X, I'd be interested to hear what you think about this.
4 Maybe we're digressing a little.
5 If I could just bring the conversation back to the agenda.
6 I'd like to draw things to a close.
7 Can I just ask everyone to sum up their views?

Further practice

If students need more practice, go to *Practice file 4* on page 108 of the *Student's Book*.

CULTURE QUESTION

Students can discuss these questions in pairs before comparing answers with the rest of the class. You might like to raise the point that whether people interrupt or not can often depend on who is talking – you might be less likely to interrupt your superiors, even if they are talking about totally irrelevant issues. It may also be the case that there are far fewer interruptions in Eastern cultures, as decisions there are more often based on harmony and consensus, rather than argument and debate.

Exercise 7

Students should work in groups with people from the same company or line of work. If this isn't possible, you should follow the activity on page 138 of the *Student's Book*. You may even choose to do both if you have time. Allow students time to prepare before they hold the teleconference and encourage them to use language from the *Key expressions*. If you have the opportunity, you could use real teleconferencing equipment.

After the task, give positive feedback to students who included a lot of the target language. Note any expressions used incorrectly during the teleconference and ask students to correct them without looking at the *Key expressions*. You could also ask if they felt there was adequate turn-taking during the teleconference, or if the interruptions were excessive.

PRE-WORK LEARNERS If you would prefer not to do the activity on page 138 of the *Student's Book*, then you could write the alternative topics below on the board. Students work in groups and choose one topic to discuss in their teleconference. Ask them to identify three or four issues for their chosen subject. Allow plenty of time for students to prepare their ideas.

- *How to improve the health and fitness of people in your community*
- *How to improve the education system in your country*
- *How to improve the quality of TV programmes in your country*
- *How to make your town more environmentally-friendly*

ONE-TO-ONE Ask the student to tell you about something that is under discussion in their company at the moment. Then set up a two-way phone call with the student to discuss the topic. You play the role of a colleague from an office in a different area who has been brought in to help. They have to bring you up-to-date on the latest developments. Ask the student to use as many of the *Key expressions* as possible, for example, inviting you to say something, expressing doubts, etc.

Photocopiable worksheet

Download and photocopy *Unit 4 Business communication worksheet* from the teacher resources in the *Online practice*.

Language at work

Exercise 1

Write the words *this* and *that* on the board. Then write the following sentences on the board:

Is that the report you want me to read before the meeting?

No, this is the one I meant.

This is Liz speaking. Is that Jorge?

Ask students if they can explain when you normally use *this* and when you use *that*. (It relates to perceived distance from the speaker – physically in these examples, but also metaphorically in others.) Then ask students to work in pairs, read audio script 4.2 on page 148, and identify the meaning of the underlined pronouns in the sentences.

Answers

1 *That* refers to the comment the speaker has just made. *It* refers to the subject related to the comment.
2 *This* is the subject under discussion. *That* refers to the exploration of a proposed solution last year. *It* was the solution proposed.
3 *This* is the subject under discussion.
4 *This* is the proposal the speaker is about to make.
5 The first *that* refers to the point that has been reached in the discussion. The second *that* refers to what the speaker is saying.
6 *It* refers to the suggestion just made.
7 The first *it* refers to the decision-making process. The second *it* refers to the subject the speaker is about to talk about.

Exercise 2

Ask students to refer to sentences 2 and 4 in **1**. Elicit the answers to the questions from the whole class.

Answers
1 that
2 this

Grammar reference

If students need more information, go to *Grammar reference* on page 128 of the *Student's Book*.

Exercise 3

Students choose the correct words. Ask individual students to read the sentences aloud. Point out that we normally stress *this* and *that*, but not *it*.

Answers
1 That	4 that
2 That	5 this
3 It	6 It

PRONUNCIATION Write the following sentences on the board and elicit the difference in pronunciation of *that*.

That's interesting.

I don't think that there's an easy solution.

In the first case, *that* /ðæt/ is stressed (strong form), because it's an emphatic pronoun. In the second, *that* is unstressed (weak form) /ðət/ so the vowel is pronounced as a schwa /ə/.

Now write the following sentences on the board and ask students to identify whether the strong or weak form of the words in bold would be used (answers are in brackets).

1 ***That's*** *the right one.* (strong)
2 ***It*** *comes from Serbia.* (weak)
3 *What's **it** for?* (weak)
4 ***It**'s for saving data.* (weak)
5 *Who do I give **that** to?* (strong)
6 *Send **it** to me.* (weak)
7 *Why did you do **that**?* (strong)
8 *Is **this** the one you meant to send?* (strong)
9 *Whose idea was **it**?* (weak)
10 *Yes, **that** caused a problem for the company.* (strong)

Exercise 4

Students add the missing pronouns to the conversation. They can check their answers with a partner.

Suggested answers
Jorge According to <u>this</u> report, sales of our new PXD tools have gone up 22%.
Cerys <u>That's</u> excellent news. <u>It's</u> been a long time since we sold so many.
Jorge <u>That's</u> true, but have you seen <u>this</u>? <u>It's</u> a review of market prospects over the next 5 years and <u>it's</u> not encouraging.
Cerys No, <u>that's</u> not one I've seen. What does <u>it</u> say? Is <u>it</u> suggesting that the market's slowing?
Jorge <u>That's</u> about right.
Cerys I've read a number of recent articles saying <u>that</u>.
Jorge <u>That's</u> quite depressing. <u>It</u> makes me wonder if <u>it's</u> time to get out of <u>this</u> market.
Cerys I think <u>it's</u> a good idea to call a meeting. <u>This is</u> something we need to discuss.

Further practice

If students need more practice, go to *Practice file 4* on page 109 of the *Student's Book*.

Exercise 5

Students choose a topic and then discuss it with a partner. Encourage them to use referencing language in their conversations. Monitor and make a note of any incorrect uses of *it*, *this* and *that*. Give feedback on this after the activity.

PRE-WORK LEARNERS Write the following alternative topics on the board:

* *a current story in this week's newspaper*
* *a recent film you've seen*
* *something happening in your town*
* *something happening in your place of study*

Ask students to work with a partner, choose a topic and discuss it, using reference language were possible.

Photocopiable worksheet

Download and photocopy *Unit 4 Language at work worksheet* from the teacher resources in the *Online practice*.

Practically speaking

Exercise 1

Students complete the activity in pairs. Discuss the possible answers with the whole class. You may need to give an example for option g:

A *I work in publishing.*
B *Publishing?*

And an example for option j:

A *Going down the Amazon was a real nightmare.*
B *In what way was it a nightmare?*

Possible answers
1 c, d, e, g, j
2 a, b, c, f, g, h, i, j
3 b, c, e, f, g, j

Exercise 2

▶ **4.4** Students listen and complete the table. Remind them to refer to the methods listed in **1**. Ask them to compare their notes with a partner before comparing answers with the rest of the class.

Answers

Extract	Relationship	Methods	Phrases
1	1st meeting, colleagues in same company, different locations	d, e	It's Steve, isn't it? I've seen your picture on the website. How was the journey?
2	old colleagues	b, c, e, h	You're looking well. I thought I recognized that voice. I may be old, but you can't get rid of me that easily. And are you still enjoying it?
3	old colleagues	a, e, g	It must be two years or more since we last met. Wasn't it at that conference in … Oh yes, … it was really beautiful, … do you remember …? Someone said you'd had a difficult year. (Yes. I have had a few ups and downs.) Ups and downs?
4	colleagues who haven't met before	b, e, i	You're not the Janos that pulled off that big Integra deal, are you? Well, it wasn't just me. There was a whole team involved. And anyway, Pietro, I've heard quite a lot about you, too. You got the gold award last month, didn't you?
5	old colleagues	f, j	Well, I'd been working … when senior management decided … So I've been … the job's pretty challenging. But I'm enjoying it. Challenging in what way?

Useful phrases

Refer students to the *Useful phrases* section on page 134 of the *Student's Book* for extension and revision.

Exercise 3

Refer students to the methods for establishing rapport in **1** and give them a few minutes to think about their future life. Point out that their imagined future doesn't necessarily have to be completely perfect – they may have had some 'ups and downs'. Make sure you also prepare for the activity. When they are ready, ask students to circulate and talk to other people. After the activity, ask students which of them seems to have had the most successful/interesting/difficult five years.

> **KEY WORD** Students match 1–7 to a–g individually. They can then compare their answers in pairs before comparing answers with the rest of the class.
>
> **Answers**
> **1** b **2** a **3** e **4** d **5** g **6** c **7** f

PRONUNCIATION Ask students to look at the key word *matter*, and decide if it's the main stressed word in each phrase or not (the stressed words are in bold):

Answers
What's the matter?
It's **no** laughing matter.
We'll do it, no matter **what**.
That will make matters **worse**.
As a matter of fact, I **do** smoke.
This **matters**.
It's a matter of **urgency**.

Progress test

Download and photocopy *Unit 4 Progress test* and *Speaking test* from the teacher resources in the *Online practice*.

Talking point

Discussion

ALTERNATIVE Before students read the articles, you could ask them to think of recent Olympic Games, Summer and/or Winter, or any other international sporting event, and any problems that occurred or concerns expressed before the games. Ask them if the problems actually did affect the games, or disappeared when people got involved in the event. You could also ask them if they thought that holding Olympic Games has a positive or negative effect on the area, or no effect at all. If they don't know very much about this topic, you could ask them to look up previous Olympics or find out more about them.

Exercise 1

Allow time for students to read the two articles and be prepared to answer any questions about vocabulary.

You may need to check students' understanding of the following:

scrap = to get rid of something

plagiarise = to copy another person's ideas, words or work and pretend that they are your own

scaled-down = reduced in number, size or extent

spiralling = a continuous harmful increase or decrease in something, that gradually gets faster and faster

Students discuss the question in pairs, before comparing answers with the rest of the class.

> **Answers**
> Plagiarism allegations: The committee could have double-checked other logos. This is relatively easily done online. Spiralling costs: The committee could have set a limit on possible spend on the stadium before Hadid was given the commission. They should also have kept an eye on the costs throughout the process.

Exercise 2

Students work with a partner. They read the difficulties and decide what could have been done to avoid the risks. If you think they need help coming up with answers, it might be a good idea to do the first problem with the whole class and then ask them to complete the rest of the table.

Task

Exercise 1

Students work in small groups. They decide on a list of five things that could go wrong when planning a big national or global event, for example, unforeseen costs; building delays; transport infrastructure problems; lack of facilities for spectators; ticket sales lower than expected; not enough sponsors; weather problems; etc.

Exercise 2

Students work in their groups. They hold a meeting, make a decision on the event, and work through the questions. Ask all students to make notes recording what is discussed in the meeting.

When they have prepared their answers, split the groups and team students with people from other groups to present their ideas. You could ask them to write an agenda and nominate a chairperson before the meeting. You could also decide to organize the meeting as if it were a teleconference. In this case, refer students to the *Key expressions* in *Business communication* on page 33 before they have their meeting.

When getting feedback from the whole class, write the following questions on the board:

- *Were all the participants in the meeting equally involved in the discussion? Why/Why not?*
- *Did you reach an agreement on the event to be staged and what should be done to make sure it is successful? Why/Why not?*

Ask students to answer the questions in their group before comparing answers with the class and discussing how successful each meeting was.

EXTENSION For homework, students could either write up the minutes of their meeting, or they could write a report based on what ideas were recommended and what ideas were rejected, and why.

ONE-TO-ONE You can ask the student to present his/her plan for a large international event. Ask him/her to assess the risks and make suggestions on how the risks can be avoided.

5 Teamwork

Context

Teamwork is important in our everyday lives. Most jobs involve an element of teamwork and your students are likely to have experienced working in both good and bad teams. Good teamwork is integral to the success of a project or a company. It can also increase levels of job satisfaction for employees, as it enables close working relationships to develop and each team member can feel they have a significant role to play.

In a successful team, ideas are shared freely, and all members of the team are committed to working towards a common goal and to giving each other supportive feedback. Clear leadership within the team is the key to success. However, problems can arise if there is a lack of strategy or focus. Poor communication between team leaders and their team can lead to de-motivation. At the same time, divisions within teams can result from clashes of personality, different working styles or sometimes cultural clashes.

Many businesses recognize how difficult effective teamworking is, and attempt to enhance their employees' collaborative efforts through workshops and training. Dr Meredith Belbin is a British researcher and management theorist, best known for his work on management teams..This unit includes a reading based on his research. He proposes nine team roles required for successful teams. In this unit, students have the opportunity to discuss team relationships in connection to these roles. They then focus on the language used when dealing with conflict and when emphasizing a point of view. In the *Talking point*, they evaluate a teamwork problem and discuss ways to improve it.

Starting point

Discuss the questions as a class. It might be a good idea to dictate the *Starting point* questions and have students work with the books closed so they don't look at the headings in the text before they answer the questions. Ask students to think about the different roles that people play within teams, for example, a coordinator or an evaluator. Write any ideas on the board.

Possible answers
1 Team members don't get on; they have different working styles; some people are unreliable; there may be a clash of objectives; some people don't participate enough.
2 Students' own answers

ALTERNATIVE Ask students to think of their favourite sports team (e.g. football, basketball, etc.) and ask them if it's a good team or not, and why/why not? Then write the following quote on the board and ask students to discuss how far they agree with it.

'Talent wins games, but teamwork and intelligence win championships.' Michael Jordan, US basketball player

Then hand out large sheets of paper with the word *teamwork* on them. Ask students to work in small groups and brainstorm what teamwork means to them. When they have finished, ask students to walk around and look at other groups' ideas.

PRE-WORK LEARNERS Ask students to work in small groups and to think of projects where they have worked in teams during their studies, and discuss the following questions:

- What advantages are there to working in a team?
- Did they experience any disadvantages to working in a team, and if so, what were they?
- What sort of people are the most useful in a teamwork situation?
- Are there any types of personality that don't work well in a team?
- Do they prefer to work in a team or on their own? Ask them to give reasons for their answer.

Working with words

Exercise 1

Students read the text and compare the team roles with their ideas in *Starting point*. Before they read, you might want to check that students understand the following:

absent-minded = tending to forget things, often due to being unfocused/thinking about other things
boundless = without limits
thrive = prosper, make good progress

Exercise 2

Students read the text again and discuss the questions with a partner.

Answers

1 **Plant:** + innovative and finds solutions, – not good at communication

Resource Investigator: + enthusiastic at the start, excellent networker, – loses momentum later on

Co-ordinator: + able to see the bigger picture, good at delegating, – sometimes neglects own work

Shaper: + motivates teams, pushes others hard, thrives on pressure, – can upset others by not considering their feelings

Teamworker: + good listener, – not good at making decisions

Completer Finisher: + good attention to detail, – poor delegator, over-emphasis on minor details

Monitor Evaluator: + logical, able to judge situations, – lacks the enthusiasm to inspire others

Implementer: + disciplined, performs consistently, – no deviation, finds it difficult to incorporate new ideas

Specialist: + highly skilled and knowledgeable, – focuses on technicalities

2 Students' own answers

EXTRA ACTIVITY

Dictate the adjectives below. Ask students to work with a partner and put the adjectives into two groups: one group for positive adjectives and one group for negative adjectives.

careless, opportunistic, thorough, arrogant, tolerant, caring, irresponsible, prudent, pushy, ruthless, supportive, controlling, bullying, attentive, helpful, enterprising, confrontational, obsessive, confident, uncaring, humorous, nosey, ambitious, indecisive, open to change, interfering, understanding, lazy, fair, passive, assertive, cheerful, flexible, aggressive, persevering, energetic, nit-picking, demanding, moody, curious

Answers

Positive

thorough, tolerant, caring, prudent, supportive, attentive, helpful, enterprising, confident, humorous, *ambitious, open to change, understanding, fair, assertive, cheerful, flexible, persevering, energetic, *demanding, curious

Negative

careless, opportunistic, arrogant, irresponsible, pushy, ruthless, controlling, bullying, confrontational, obsessive, uncaring, nosey, indecisive, interfering, lazy, passive, aggressive, nit-picking, moody

*Note that these adjectives could also be considered to be negative.

When they have made their lists, ask students to check they understand the meaning of the adjectives. They should look up any unfamiliar words in a dictionary. As you monitor, check they can pronounce each one correctly. Then ask them to use the adjectives to describe a team they have worked in to their partner.

DICTIONARY SKILLS

Ask students to choose five positive and five negative adjectives. Tell them to check in their dictionary where the stress in the adjectives is.

Then, with a partner, ask them to give a definition of each of the words and their partner says which word it is. They have to make sure their partner is pronouncing the word correctly.

EXTENSION If your students are interested in Belbin and his theories, ask them to research him online.

Exercise 3

Students underline the correct adverbs and then check their answers in the text in **1**.

Answers

1	effectively	6	logically
2	vigorously	7	periodically
3	carefully	8	objectively
4	hard	9	consistently
5	excessively	10	positively

Exercise 4

Students work in pairs and share advice on how to have successful working relationships using the verb + adverb combinations in **3**.

Possible answers

1 The best managers can *communicate* their ideas *effectively*.

2 The sales team was really successful because they *vigorously pursued the opportunities* the new market provided.

3 If you are working with a difficult and demanding boss, you should always *tread carefully* with him/her.

4 If a manager *pushes* his/her team too *hard*, he/she will find they begin to become less efficient.

5 If you *worry excessively about minor details*, you will never be able to see the bigger picture – the task as a whole.

6 In order to come up with a workable solution to the problem, it is essential to *analyse the situation logically*.

7 When implementing change in any organization, it is a good idea to build in times when the team in charge of change management can *analyse the situation periodically*, and make any necessary adjustments.

8 To get the best solution to a problem, it is advisable to *look at* all the available options *objectively* before making a decision.

9 Annual appraisals are a way a company can assess whether staff are *performing consistently in their roles* and if they are not, give them goals to aim for to achieve their objectives.

10 If you want to be *viewed positively*, make sure you meet all your deadlines.

PRE-WORK LEARNERS Ask students to talk about successful relationships with people they're studying with. What do they think are the most important things that make a successful relationship? Alternatively, they can refer to relationships they have had with colleagues during work placements.

Exercise 5

▶ 5.1 Students listen and identify the strengths and weaknesses of each person. Students can then compare their notes in pairs, before comparing answers with the rest of the class.

Possible answers
Speaker 1 Strengths: ambitious, energetic, efficient, enthusiastic
Weaknesses: demanding, pushy
Speaker 2 Strengths: thorough, quick, good product knowledge
Weaknesses: doesn't delegate
Speaker 3 Strengths: methodical, thorough, reliable
Weaknesses: not open to change, can't move from brief, not flexible

Exercise 6

Students decide which Belbin role best fits each of the speakers in **5**. Refer them back to the text in **1** to remind them of the roles.

Answers
Speaker 1 Shaper
Speaker 2 Completer Finisher
Speaker 3 Implementer

Exercise 7

Students work in pairs and discuss which of the three people they would choose to work with and why.

PRE-WORK LEARNERS Write the following question on the board and ask students to answer it in pairs.

Which of the three people would you prefer as your future boss? Why?

Exercise 8

Students replace the underlined words with a multi-word verb from the text in **1**.

Answers
1 pay attention to
2 coping with
3 spurred (the rep team) into action
4 steer clear of
5 thrive on
6 focus on
7 deviated from
8 be relied on

Further practice
If students need more practice, go to *Practice file 5* on page 110 of the *Student's Book*.

Exercise 9

Students work in pairs and describe a colleague/team leader they have worked with using vocabulary from **3** and **8**. They can then discuss any similarities/differences.

This could be a sensitive topic if students are from the same company, in which case you might like to avoid this activity.

PRE-WORK LEARNERS Ask students to work in groups. They are about to start a new project and need to get a team of four to six people together. Ask them to describe the people they would like to have on the team. Ask them to give reasons for their choices.

Compare the different groups' teams. Are there some people who are in every team? Why do they think that would be the case?

Exercise 10

Students work in pairs and take turns to ask and answer questions about recent projects they have worked on. If students haven't had much experience of teamwork, ask them to turn to page 139 of the *Student's Book* and discuss the best combination of people for the team. Encourage students to use new vocabulary from this section where appropriate.

Monitor and make a note of any good use of vocabulary. If appropriate, make a note of any errors. Provide feedback after the activity and write any mistakes on the board for the class to correct.

EXTENSION Write the following questions on the board and ask students to discuss them in small groups.

- *Should the Belbin team roles model be used in a company's recruitment process? Why/Why not?*
- *Do you think it's realistic for companies to put teams together that include a balance of the Belbin roles?*
- *Have you ever had a bad teamworking experience? If so, what went wrong and why?*

Photocopiable worksheet
Download and photocopy *Unit 5 Working with words worksheet* from the teacher resources in the *Online practice*.

Business communication

Exercise 1

Ask students to read the *Context* relating to Duverger. Then ask them to discuss the questions in pairs, before comparing answers with the rest of the class. Write their ideas on the board.

Possible answers
What can go wrong: wrong photograph or logo; typographical errors; wrong content/information; colours not right; wrong font; paper quality not right; wrong quantity; etc.
Why this might happen: sample not carefully checked by someone in the company; sample not given; company changed mind about design but this wasn't communicated to printer; rushed job; printer not reliable; etc.

Exercise 2

▶ 5.2 Students listen and compare their ideas in **1** with what actually went wrong.

Answers
What went wrong: wrong logo – the logo includes a knife and they didn't want this. In addition, the quality of some of the other artwork isn't as good as it could be, and the printing should have been done months ago.
Why: Paul isn't happy because they didn't use their normal printer – they used one recommended by Riccardo. Riccardo suggests the initial artwork given to the printer wasn't up to scratch, and that perhaps the printer didn't have the latest versions of the files. Riccardo says it was a rushed job because Paul's approval of prices wasn't given until late.

Exercise 3

▶ **5.2** Students listen again and answer the questions.

Answers

1	Jenny	3	Riccardo
2	Jenny	4	Paul

Exercise 4

Student match expressions a–i to categories 1–4 in **3**. They can then compare their answers in pairs and add any other expressions they can think of.

Answers

1	a, b, g	3	c, h
2	d, e	4	f, i

Possible expressions

a   Do you get what I mean? Have I made myself clear?
b   I got the impression that … I thought that …
c   Have you been updated about …? Have you been told …? Do you know about …?
d   Let's try to stay objective. We should be professional about this.
e   Let's not get distracted by … I think we need to keep to the point here …
f   This isn't OK for me. I really don't think this is right.
g   Can I just check here, what you mean is …? Did you mean …?
h   My main concern is … I'm rather uneasy about …
i   What we should be concentrating on is … The main thing we must remember is …

Exercise 5

Students work in pairs and have the conversations. Encourage them to use expressions from **4**.

Exercise 6

▶ **5.3** Students listen and answer the questions in pairs.

Answers

1   Reprint the brochures or use the brochures as they are.
2   Riccardo is put in charge of speaking to the printer, with the possibility of organizing a reprint and changing the logo.

Exercise 7

Students answer the questions in pairs.

Answers

a   Jenny
b   Paul and Riccardo
c   Riccardo

Exercise 8

▶ **5.3** Ask students to read expressions 1–10 and think about possible alternatives to the sections in italics. They then listen again and note expressions in extract 2 with similar meanings. Ask them to compare their answers in pairs before comparing answers with the rest of the class.

Answers

1   how do you propose we deal with this issue
2   I'm sorry, but I can't just
3   I just don't understand how you could even
4   I see what you mean, but
5   I just won't be able to go ahead with
6   can we try to avoid
7   I'm prepared to overlook
8   look, would it help if I gave
9   I need to know we've got
10 can I leave you to

EXTRA ACTIVITY

Dictate or write the following six pairs of alternative expressions on the board. In pairs, students decide on the differences in tone between the alternatives. As a class, ask students to explain them (answers are in brackets). You could ask them who they would use each phrase with, for example, a colleague, their boss, a supplier, etc.

1   *a What do you think we should do about …?*
    b How do you propose we deal with …?
    (a is more informal)
2   *a Don't expect me to …*
    b I'm sorry, but I can't just …
    (b is more diplomatic)
3   *a I'm cancelling the launch …*
    b I just won't be able to go ahead with the launch …
    (a is much more direct)
4   *a I don't want any setbacks …*
    b Can we try to avoid any setbacks …?
    (b is much more diplomatic)
5   *a Why don't I give …?*
    b Would it help if I gave …?
    (a is much more direct)
6   *a Would you be happy to liaise …?*
    b Can I leave you to liaise …?
    (b is more direct)

Exercise 9

Students match the expressions they noted in **8** to a–c in **7**.

Answers

a   1, 6, 9, 10
b   2, 3, 4, 5
c   7, 8

Further practice

If students need more practice, go to *Practice file 5* on page 110 of the *Student's Book*.

Exercise 10

Students work in groups of three. Student A reads the information on page 41; Student B turns to page 141 and Student C to page 143 in the *Student's Book* and they read their information. When all three students are ready, they should discuss each situation and find a solution. Encourage them to use language from the *Key expressions*. Monitor and make notes of any errors.

At the end of the activity, ask groups to give feedback on their meetings. How did they deal with the conflict? Then write any errors on the board for the class to correct.

ONE-TO-ONE Ask the student to either choose a situation from their own company or choose one of the situations in **10**, perhaps Student A Situation 1, Student B Situation 1 on page 141 of the *Student's Book* or Student C Situation 2 on page 143. You play one of the other student's roles in each situation. Ask the student to negotiate the steps outlined in **10**. Remind him/her to use the *Key expressions* where possible.

At the end of the role-play, ask the student how they felt during the points of disagreement, and why.

> **CULTURE QUESTION**
> Students discuss the questions in pairs. Answers will vary, although the discussion may include the fact that some cultures place a high value on consensus, and this often leads to an avoidance of conflict. Conversely, in many Western cultures it is expected that people will voice their opinions, even if this results in conflict.

Photocopiable worksheet
Download and photocopy *Unit 5 Business communication worksheet* from the teacher resources in the *Online practice*.

Language at work

Exercise 1

Students underline the phrases used to add emphasis to sentences 1–8.

> **Answers**
> 1 The reason I say this is because if we get it right this time, any future campaigns should run more smoothly.
> 2 Which is why this whole thing is so frustrating.
> 3 How we resolve this is the issue now.
> 4 It's the Vienna convention which really worries me.
> 5 In which case, Riccardo, can I leave you to liaise with the printer?
> 6 What concerns me is the way this has been handled so badly by the printers.
> 7 The problems with the artwork I'm prepared to overlook.
> 8 The thing that bothers me is that we just don't have time.

Exercise 2

Students match the sentences in **1** to the techniques. Ask them to underline any fixed phrases and adverbs of degree that add emphasis. Remind them that more than one technique could be used in each sentence. (If students are unfamiliar with these techniques, you could refer them to *Grammar reference* on page 128 of the *Student's Book* before they attempt this activity.)

> **Answers**
> a 4, 6
> b 1 (The reason I say this is …), 2 (Which is why …), 5 (In which case …), 6 (What concerns me is …), 8 (The thing that bothers me is …)
> c 3, 4, 7

Grammar reference
If students need more information, go to *Grammar reference* on page 128 of the *Student's Book.*

Exercise 3

Students work in pairs and add emphasis to B's reply in conversations 1–5 using phrases from the list.

> **Possible answers**
> 1 *In which case*, wouldn't it be a good idea to sit down and sort this out properly?
> 2 *Which is why* I told you to book early.
> 3 *What we must be clear about is* it's absolutely essential that the contract is signed by the 5th.
> 4 *What I'd really like to know is* what'll happen to the team if the project is abandoned.
> 5 *It's* the changes *which* make the job interesting.

Exercise 4

Students add emphasis to the sentences using the fronting technique.

> **Answers**
> 1 How we go about this is what we need to think about.
> 2 Getting this right is absolutely crucial.

> **EXTRA ACTIVITY**
> Ask students to work in small groups and write five more sentences using the fronting technique. The groups then compare their lists and decide which sentences would be particularly effective.

EXTENSION Ask students to bring in examples of emails in English they have been sent at work. In the next lesson, ask students to work in small groups and rewrite sections of the emails, using techniques to add emphasis.

Further practice
If students need more practice, go to *Practice file 5* on page 111 of the *Student's Book.*

Exercise 5

Students work in groups of three. Allow time for them to read the information in the *Student's Book*; Student A on page 138, Student B on page 141 and Student C on page 140. They can then think about the techniques they will use to emphasize their points. When they are ready, they should have the meeting, following the points on the agenda. Monitor the use of techniques for emphasizing. Give feedback on this at the end of the activity.

ONE-TO-ONE Ask the student to choose one of the roles and you choose one of the others. Have a meeting where the student gives his/her opinions on the points on the agenda. Remind him/her to use techniques from **3** to emphasize the points he/she wants to make. Ask the student to end the meeting by deciding how you both are going to resolve the issues.

EXTENSION You could ask each group to report back on their meeting's outcomes. Or ask students to write an email to an absent colleague about what happened at the meeting.

Photocopiable worksheet

Download and photocopy *Unit 5 Language at work worksheet* from the teacher resources in the *Online practice*.

Practically speaking

Exercise 1

Students work in pairs and discuss the questions. Ask students for examples of situations at work or home where they give or receive feedback or criticism.

This could be a sensitive issue. How we react to feedback depends on how it is given, our personality and how we feel about the person giving the feedback. If your students are all from the same company, you might want to discuss these questions fairly quickly as a class.

Possible answers
1 Feedback is part of the normal process of ongoing improvement and it can be positive or negative. Criticism tends to be negative, but it can also be helpful.
2 Feedback should be fair and specific. It should also be balanced – positive comments should also be made during a feedback session.
3 Students' own answers

Exercise 2

▶ **5.4** Students listen and answer the questions.

Answers
1 Conversation 3
2 Conversation 1
3 Conversation 2

Exercise 3

▶ **5.4** Students match phrases a–k to categories 1–3 in **2**. They can then compare their answers with a partner before listening again to check.

Answers
a 3 b 1 c 2 d 2 e 3 f 3 g 3 h 1 i 2 j 2 k 3

Useful phrases

Refer students to the *Useful phrases* section on page 135 of the *Student's Book* for extension and revision.

Exercise 4

Students work in pairs and discuss appropriate responses to the feedback. Encourage them to use phrases in **3**.

Possible answers
1 Thanks for your support – it's good to know I'm on the right track.
2 Thanks! Though I have to admit, George and I worked on them together.
3 Look, you're entitled to your opinion, but I think it's just that you disagree with my findings rather than the quality of the report.
4 I'm sorry. I didn't realize that. I'll talk to them.
5 So how do you think we can improve it?
6 I see what you're saying, but the delay wasn't actually caused by us.

EXTENSION Ask students to walk around the classroom and practise the conversations in **4** with different people.

Exercise 5

Students work with a partner and read the information in the *Student's Book*. Student A turns to page 140, and Student B to page 141. They then take turns to give feedback and respond. Whilst monitoring, pay particular attention to intonation. Do students sound diplomatic/polite? Give feedback on this after the activity.

KEY WORD

Students match the phrases to suitable synonyms for *only*.

Answers
1 e 2 a 3 d 4 c 5 b

Progress test

Download and photocopy *Unit 5 Progress test* and *Speaking test* from the teacher resources in the *Online practice*.

Talking point

Discussion

Exercise 1

This *Talking point* examines a form of psychometric profiling, the Myers-Briggs Type Indicator (MBTI®). The aim of this form of assessment is to help teams solve problems more effectively and make better decisions.

Allow a few minutes for students to read the article. Be prepared to answer any questions about vocabulary. Before they read, you might want to check that students understand the following:

psychometric profiling = a system of collecting information about somebody so that you can measure their mental abilities and processes

Students answer the question for themselves and then they can discuss their answer in pairs. Ask students how useful they think the tests are, and if people can learn to 'cheat', i.e. work out what answers are being sought.

PRE-WORK LEARNERS Write the following questions on the board and ask students to discuss them in small groups.

- *Have you ever done a test like this? If so, when and what did you learn from doing it?*
- *How would you feel doing a similar test? Why?*
- *Do you think that tests like this are useful? How?*
- *Do you think you can 'cheat' or work out what answers you should give and so make the test less useful?*

Exercise 2

Ask students to discuss with a partner what they think their main personality traits are. You could ask them to think of three adjectives to describe themselves and give reasons why they chose them, and examples of how they have demonstrated them. Ask them how these traits affect their ability to solve problems.

Exercise 3

Ask students to answer these questions with a partner.

When students have discussed all three *Discussion* questions, you could have a brief whole-class discussion on interesting points that have come up.

Task

Exercise 1

Students read Shawn Bakker's recommendations for problem-solving with teams made up of different preferences. The questions are based on the model developed by Isabel Briggs Myers which was outlined in the article. With a partner, they can decide whether they think the recommendations are useful, how well they think these would work in teams in their company, and give reasons for their answers.

PRE-WORK LEARNERS Ask students to imagine they are in a team, for example, a sports team. The team is going through difficulties, for example, the sports team is losing more matches than it wins. Ask the team to use the four steps in the model developed by Isabel Briggs Myers in the article in **1** and decide whether this approach would work for the team.

When students have gone through the model, ask them to share with the class how useful, or not, this approach could be.

Exercise 2

Students work individually. They think of a problem they are facing at work and write their answers to the questions in column 2 in the table. They can refer back to the model in **1** and the article for help.

PRE-WORK LEARNERS Ask students to work individually at first and think of a different situation where they might work in a team, for example, on an academic project or organizing an event. They can then think of a problem that could arise, complete the questions from the model in **1**, and be prepared to present the problem to their group and ask for advice.

Exercise 3

Students work in groups. Each student presents his/her problem to the rest of the group and asks for advice. Then the group discusses the problems and solutions.

Monitor, noting down three good uses of the language in the unit and three errors. Write these on the board and ask students to decide which are correct and to correct the ones they think are wrong. Give any appropriate feedback on use of language.

> **EXTRA ACTIVITY**
>
> Ask students to write up the problems and solutions discussed in their group, and email them to you. Provide feedback in the next lesson.
>
> Alternatively, you could ask students to write up the problems and solutions in different emails. Then you could make copies of a problem email from each group and ask the other groups to come up with a solution. When they have done that, you can present the original solution and compare.

ONE-TO-ONE The student can read the *Context* and article, and then you can do the *Discussion* questions together. Ask him/her how he/she feels about the usefulness of psychometric testing, and if their company ever uses it. For the *Task* you can discuss and comment on his/her problems and comments. During the preparation stage, encourage your student to add any of his/her own ideas, and relate it to their own situation.

Unit content

By the end of this unit, students will be able to

- discuss innovation
- talk about new ideas and use adverbs
- avoid giving direct answers.

Context

In today's fast-moving business environment, it's becoming more of a challenge for companies to ensure that they continue to progress and grow. Their ability to do so depends on a number of factors. One of the most important of these is creativity. Many of the companies which became leaders in their field did so because of their ability to 'think outside the box' and come up with innovative products that captured the imagination of the market, e.g. Google with its wide range of search-related services; Skype with its concept of a free Internet phone service; Apple with its novel vision of a portable multipurpose device that gave rise to the iPad.

However, progress also depends on healthy financial performance, and with the emphasis on cost-efficiency, productivity and shareholder value, today's companies have to balance the need for creativity with a more realistic economic view. This balance isn't always easy to achieve, since innovation and creativity require both time and money.

In this unit, students learn to talk about success factors and discuss the balance between creativity, profitability and quality. They practise the language of putting forward, developing, clarifying and evaluating ideas in the context of brainstorming meetings. They also look at the adverbs we use to indicate different attitudes, and language for expressing vagueness. In the *Viewpoint* they watch a video on ethical consumption and being a conscientious consumer.

Starting point

Briefly brainstorm ways in which scientific innovations have improved the world in the last 20 years.

Possible answers
Transport: electric vehicles (cars, buses), faster trains and planes
Medicine: new drugs and treatments for serious/fatal illnesses
Communications: smartphones, computer developments

Students discuss the questions in pairs before comparing answers with the rest of the class. If they work, encourage them to also think about their own company and competitors in their field when discussing the questions.

Possible answers
1 innovate, ensure best quality; benchmark against competitors; manage costs; maximize profit margins to be able to invest in new products; employ the best people; be flexible – offering different employment contracts; advertise widely
2 avoid complacency; seek to continuously improve; recognize mistakes and act on them quickly; avoid stretching company resources (financial or human); stay in touch with rapidly changing consumer tastes/demands and with new technology

Working with words

Exercise 1

As a lead-in, write *3M – Science. Applied to Life* on the board. Ask students what they know about the company 3M and what it does. (According to its website *3M is a science-based technology company committed to improving lives and doing business in the right way.* It is actually a multinational conglomerate and has many divisions including automotive, transportation, electronics, healthcare and energy.) Students then read the quote, and discuss as a class what concerns the company might have faced. Ask if they agree with George Buckley's views on creativity.

Possible answers
The quote implies that under a strict quality control regime, coming up with new, innovative ideas would need to be measured against a set quota (*quota* = a fixed amount of something someone needs to achieve), but that this is problematic because it is impossible to predict when flashes of inspiration will occur.

Exercise 2

Students read the text and answer the questions. Then they discuss their answers with a partner.

Answers
1 He introduced the 'Six Sigma' process.
2 It was initially successful, but later caused problems.
3 Top level management should be involved directly and enthusiastically in implementing any changes. The diversity within the company should be recognized and taken into consideration, and different approaches to change may be necessary for different teams.

Exercise 3

Students match phrases 1–6 from the text in **2** to definitions a–f. They can then compare their answers with a partner.

Answers
1 c 2 d 3 f 4 e 5 a 6 b

Exercise 4

Students look back at the text in **2** and replace the underlined words in the sentences with a verb phrase in bold from the text. Remind students they may have to change the form of the verb phrase.

Note that *try out, figure out* and *bounce around* are separable so a noun/noun phrase can also separate the phrasal verb. For example, both *I'm trying different things out* and *I'm trying out different things* are possible. However, if a pronoun is used, it must separate the phrasal verb, e.g. *try it out,* not *try out it.*

Answers
1 try out (both are possible – *try his ideas out / try out his ideas*)
2 run into
3 figure out (more likely not to split this as the object is too long)
4 look beyond
5 hit on
6 bounce around (both are possible – *bounce the ideas around / bounce around the ideas*)

Exercise 5

Students work with a partner. Ask them if they can remember which nouns collocate with the verb phrases from the article in **2**. They can then check their answers in the text. Then ask them to think of other nouns that collocate with the verb phrases.

Answers (and possible answers)
1 ideas (suggestions, proposals)
2 mistakes (the horizon, the present situation)
3 the idea (a solution)
4 difficulty (problems, a snag)
5 things (a scheme, a proposal, an idea)
6 tensions (the situation, the amount, the cost)

Exercise 6

Students use phrases from **3** and **4** to tell their partner about an idea they came up with at work.

PRE-WORK LEARNERS Ask students to think about when they or their class/study group came up with an idea to improve their approach to their studies. If they have never done this, then ask them to list two or three problems they have when studying and come up with some ideas on how to improve their situation.

Exercise 7

▶ **6.1** Students listen to a business analyst talking about the situation at 3M and make notes about the three headings.

Before students listen, you might want to elicit the meanings of the following:

the bottom line = the amount of money that is a profit or loss after everything has been calculated; can also be the most important thing that you have to consider or accept, the essential point in a discussion, etc.

knock something into shape = to make something more acceptable, organized or successful, not necessarily gently
an efficiency drive = an organized effort to make the company efficient
stifle creativity = to prevent creativity from happening

Answers
Before McNerney's leadership: creative, innovative; not in good financial shape
During McNerney's leadership: boost earnings; cut workforce by 11%; shareholder pleasing; shift focus from creativity to quality control; eliminate production defects
During George Buckley's leadership: reeling back on Six Sigma just enough to get the creative juices flowing again

EXTENSION Ask your students what they already know about the Six Sigma strategy. (It's a business management strategy that was first introduced by Motorola in the 1980s and was designed to identify and remove causes of defects and errors in manufacturing companies.) Ask them to find out more about the Six Sigma strategy before the next lesson including any advantages and disadvantages.

Exercise 8

Students work in pairs and form collocations. Don't give feedback on the answers yet.

Answers
1 the bottom line
2 change
3 the emphasis
4 earnings
5 mistakes
6 a stir
7 costs
8 the competition

Exercise 9

▶ **6.1** Students work in pairs to complete the sentences from the interview with a collocation from **8**. They then listen again and check their answers.

Answers
1 cutting into the bottom line
2 underwent, changes
3 boost earnings
4 caused quite a stir
5 tolerate mistakes easily
6 outperform the competition

Further practice

If students need more practice, go to *Practice file 6* on page 112 of the *Student's Book*.

Exercise 10

Students work in groups and discuss a recent project. Encourage them to use some of the language in **3**, **5** and **8** during their discussions. If students are not from the same team/company, you could ask them to compare and contrast different projects they have worked on. Monitor and listen out for collocations used by the different groups and make a note of who used them.

When students have finished the activity, ask questions to the whole class relating to the collocations you noted. For example:

- Which group had an idea which took a long time to *get off the ground*?
- Who *ran into problems*?
- Who had a radical idea that *caused a stir*?

The groups that used those collocations can then explain briefly to the class what happened during their project, i.e. why it took a long time to get off the ground, etc.

PRE-WORK LEARNERS Ask students to think about any projects they have been involved in. This could be:

- a group project relating to their studies
- a group presentation they had to give
- organizing an event (e.g. a party, sports event, etc.)

Photocopiable worksheet
Download and photocopy *Unit 6 Working with words worksheet* from the teacher resources in the *Online practice*.

Business communication

Exercise 1

▶ **6.2–6.4** As a lead-in, you could ask students to brainstorm ideas in pairs under the headings 'Problems faced by small shops' and 'How small shops can fight back'. Elicit answers from the class then refer them to the *Context*. Students then listen and follow the instructions in 1–2.

Ask students to compare their answers in pairs before comparing answers with the rest of the class.

Possible answers

Ideas	Pros	Cons
1 recycling of computer parts and maybe send them to developing countries	gives company a more caring image	might not be cost-effective or practical
2 volunteer training programme in developing country	rewarding experience for staff; gives company a more caring image	might not be cost-effective or practical
3 specializing in energy-saving, e.g. solar-powered laptops	big money in energy saving; could open up market share, especially through website and company could gain competitive advantage	risky – too different from present business
4 sell recovered parts through brokers or even act as brokers themselves	could be more competitive on service than brokers	not original – another company (Green PCs) already does this

Exercise 2

▶ **6.2** Students listen again to the first extract and complete the sentences.

Answers
1. couldn't we consider
2. it's not clear to me what you mean by
3. Well, for example
4. I would have thought it would be possible to
5. Oh, I see, so you're thinking of / am I right
6. Thinking about it, we could even
7. I'm not totally convinced
8. I'm concerned about how
9. I can't help wondering whether
10. I would certainly need to know / before taking it any further

Exercise 3

Students work with a partner and categorize the expressions in **2**.

Answers
a 1, 4
b 2, 5
c 3
d 6
e 7, 8, 9, 10

Exercise 4

Students work in pairs and brainstorm alternative ways of saying sentences 1–9. Encourage them to consider the real meaning behind each sentence before they start to think of alternatives.

Possible answers
1. I doubt that it would be cost-effective.
2. I've got an idea about a wider policy on environmental issues, but I'm not sure it would work and I need input from other people on this.
3. Can you explain your ideas to us?
4. What I was thinking of was solar-powered laptops.
5. What if we were to sell recovered parts back to the manufacturers?
6. There's no reason why we can't set up as brokers ourselves, is there?
7. It's a good idea. It's got potential. Let's look into this further.
8. There are a lot of drawbacks to this idea, but we shouldn't abandon it completely.
9. Regarding marketing, I think it could be a really good idea.

Further practice
If students need more practice, go to *Practice file 6* on page 112 of the *Student's Book*.

Exercise 5

Students work in groups of four. Ask them to read the information from HR before dividing the groups into two. Then allow each pair time to discuss the ideas for Students A and B on page 49 of the *Student's Book*, and for Students C and D on page 143. Each pair should choose two ideas to put forward at the meeting. Encourage them to consider the pros and cons of these two ideas and to think about how they will react if any disadvantages are mentioned during the meeting. Students should then return to their group of four and have the meeting. When they have finished, ask each group to summarize their decisions.

ONE-TO-ONE Ask the student to think about his/her own company. Ask him/her to imagine that the company's HR department is worried about staff turnover. Ask the student to think of perks that the company might be able to offer. Ask him/her to look at the following perks and choose two perks he/she thinks would be feasible for the company to offer in order to attract new staff and to hold onto existing staff:

- provide in-house gym facilities with showers
- offer staff a 'work at home' option
- offer staff the option to work their hours in three or four days, rather than five
- introduce a yearly paid bonus for all staff
- student's own suggestion

Ask the student to present their ideas. He/she should outline the advantages of the ideas and how they would work. He/she should also think of possible disadvantages and prepare a counter-argument.

Exercise 6

Ask students to work in groups of three or four. Each student chooses a work-related scenario. Ask them to focus on a problem which hasn't yet been resolved. Alternatively, they can choose one of the problems provided. Each member of the group explains their problem and they all then brainstorm possible solutions. Remind students to make use of the *Key expressions*.

Monitor during the task and make a note of three correct and three incorrect expressions students used during their discussion. After the activity, write these expressions on the board and ask the class to correct them where necessary.

ONE-TO-ONE Ask the student to think of a work-related problem he/she has had which needed a creative solution. Ask him/her to give a meeting/presentation where he/she outlines various solutions (minimum of two) that were suggested. At the meeting, you engage the student by asking for clarification. Remind the student to make use of the *Key expressions* to put forward the ideas, clarify and build on ideas, and finally to evaluate the ideas. If this is a real scenario, ask the student which solution was chosen and to give the reason for the company's choice. Alternatively, ask the student to choose one of the problems in **6** and give the presentation on that.

PRE-WORK LEARNERS Students can choose one of the two problems given. Ask them to develop the background of their imagined company a little more, e.g. what its area of activity is, what the product/service is, or what kind of employees are required.

ALTERNATIVE Ask students to work in groups of four. Write the following instructions on the board:

- *Find out which person in your group has had a work-related problem that they have already resolved.*
- *Write the details of the problem on a piece of paper, then give it to another group.*
- *Look at the problem your group has been given and brainstorm a solution to it in your group.*
- *Present the problem and your solutions to the class.*
- *Find out who had the problem and if their solution was similar to any of your suggestions.*

> **CULTURE QUESTION**
>
> Ask students to discuss the questions in pairs before comparing answers with the rest of the class. Be aware that if students are from the same company, they may find the subject matter a little sensitive, especially if there are more senior managers present. You may want to avoid the questions.

PRE-WORK LEARNERS Ask students to work in pairs and pick a famous company, either national or international, and prepare a short presentation on its 'company culture'. Ask students to find out about the company policies online.

Photocopiable worksheet

Download and photocopy *Unit 6 Business communication worksheet* from the teacher resources in the *Online practice*.

Language at work

Exercise 1

▶ **6.5** As a lead-in, write the following two sentences on the board and ask students to discuss in pairs if they are true or false (answers are in brackets).

1 All adverbs end in *-ly* (false, e.g. *well / hard / just*).

2 All adverbs qualify/describe a verb (false, they also qualify adjectives).

Students listen to adverbs being used and then match the adverbs to their uses individually before comparing their answers with a partner.

Possible answers
1 c **2** a **3** d **4** b **5** a **6** a **7** b **8** c **9** d **10** d

ALTERNATIVE Students could listen first with their books closed and note down all the adverbs they hear, before matching the adverbs to their uses.

Exercise 2

▶ **6.6** Students now listen to the pairs of sentences. You might like to pause the listening after each pair of sentences and allow the class time to discuss the difference in meaning with you.

Possible answers
1 a The speaker wants to add a bit more.
b The speaker is persuading others to listen.
2 a The speaker wasn't expecting it to be a difficult year.
b The speaker expected it to be difficult, but not as difficult as this.
3 a It was a surprise to the speaker.
b The speaker may be responding to another person who imagined the opposite would be true.
4 a The speaker is emphasizing a comment – the speaker is convinced they can't get away with it.
b The speaker is softening a negative reaction.

Grammar reference

If students need more information, go to *Grammar Reference* on page 129 of the *Student's Book*.

Exercise 3

Students work in pairs to produce appropriate responses.

Possible answers
1 Can I just run through some ideas?
2 I'm not totally convinced the money is being well spent. / I just feel that the money could be better spent elsewhere.
3 Actually, there were far more people than we expected.
4 I just can't see why we're behind schedule.
5 Yes, I was – the proposal that was accepted was easily/ obviously the best.
6 Actually, I would have gone for someone else.

Exercise 4

Students take turns to put the adverbs from **1** into sentences 1–5. Students decide what attitudes the changes express.

Answers
Students' own answers

Further practice

If students need more practice, go to *Practice file 6* on page 113 of the *Student's Book*.

Exercise 5

Ask students to decide on their favourite and least favourite technological innovation. They should then explain their choices in pairs, using as many adverbs as they can.

Monitor and note any mistakes made in the choice or placement of adverbs and write the sentences on the board for whole-class correction after the activity.

Possible answers
My favourite innovation is the MP3 player. It's *easily* the most convenient way to store your music because it's so compact and can store hundreds of songs.
My least favourite innovation is air conditioning. It's *totally* unnecessary in my country and it *actually* causes more problems than it solves – my skin and eyes become *really* dry and uncomfortable when it's on.

ALTERNATIVE You could ask students to note down the adverbs from **1** on slips of paper and place them face down in front of them. Students then talk about the innovations using the adverb they pick up.

Photocopiable worksheet

Download and photocopy *Unit 6 Language at work worksheet* from the teacher resources in the *Online practice*.

Practically speaking

Exercise 1

▶ **6.7** Students listen and answer the questions. Allow students time to discuss their answers in pairs before comparing answers with the rest of the class. You may need to check that students know the meaning of *vague* (not clear / without details).

Possible answers
Conversation 1
1 Tentative and vague, but tries to be helpful.
2 He doesn't remember the details – too long ago.

Conversation 2
1 Not specific, but encouraging, although maybe a little lazy.
2 No concrete ideas – wants to be encouraging, but doesn't want to do the work himself; probably hasn't studied the report in detail.

Conversation 3
1 vague
2 She doesn't have the photos and is struggling to put her descriptions into words.

Exercise 2

▶ **6.7** Students listen again and add more phrases to the table. You may like to point out/elicit how we can use *kind of* with a noun (*the kind of thing we're looking for*) and an adjective (*it was kind of minimalist*), and that we can replace *kind* with *sort* in both cases. Students might also like to know that we use the expression *a hint of* to describe colour, taste or your interpretation of someone's attitude (e.g. *a hint of irony*).

Answers
Conversation 1: I'm not quite sure now / I seem to remember / something like that / I'm trying to think
Conversation 2: it just needs a bit more / and so on / something along those lines / something like that
Conversation 3: it almost had a hint of / it was kind of / you know, that sort of thing / a bit like that

Useful phrases

Refer students to the *Useful phrases* section on page 135 of the *Student's Book* for extension and revision.

Exercise 3

Students work in pairs. Student A reads the information on page 51, and Student B turns to page 140. Allow them time to read the information about the situations before they have the conversations. Monitor and check they are using the phrases from **1** and **2** correctly.

Exercise 4

Students work in pairs. Each student chooses the subject they want to be asked about. Encourage students to ask fairly difficult questions (e.g. *What was the name of the trainer at the training session you went to last?*). Monitor and be ready to add a few 'difficult' questions of your own if students' memories seem a little too reliable.

PRE-WORK LEARNERS Ask students to talk about a hotel or city they have been to.

KEY WORD
Students match 1–5 with a–e. Ask them to check their answers in pairs before comparing answers with the rest of the class.

Answers
1 e 2 b 3 d 4 c 5 a

Progress test

Download and photocopy *Unit 6 Progress test* and *Speaking test* from the teacher resources in the *Online practice*.

Viewpoint 2

Exercise 1

Students work in small groups. Draw their attention to the five logos. Tell students the speaker will refer to the five companies. Before they watch the video, ask them to discuss anything they know about the companies.

Exercise 2

Tell students that phrases 1–11 come up in the video. Ask them to match phrases 1–11 to their meanings a–k.

Answers
1 c 2 i 3 g 4 f 5 j 6 b 7 k 8 e 9 d 10 h
11 a

Exercise 3

● 01 Tell students they are going to watch the first part of an interview with Hiram Samel, where he defines the terms *ethical consumption* and *conscientious consumerism*. Before students watch the video, allow them time to read the summary. You could ask students to work in pairs to try to predict the missing words, or whether they will be nouns, verbs, adjectives, etc.

Answers
1 justice	5 workers
2 system	6 living
3 floor	7 markets
4 farm	8 state

Exercise 4

● 02 Allow students to read the questions and then watch the next part of the interview. Students check their answers with a partner.

Answers
1 The state doesn't have the capacity or desire to do it. There may also be other factors which affect its motivation.
2 It depends on who runs the farm or village where the goods are produced. This is perceived as unfair.
3 Big retailers in countries like the UK make more profit from the goods than the producers do.
4 Market mechanisms are not enough – it takes political mechanisms to ensure fairness.

Exercise 5

Students work in small groups and discuss the questions. You could get students to conduct a class poll on how often their decision-making in a supermarket is affected by whether the product is ethically produced and on whether they consider themselves conscientious consumers.

Exercise 6

● 03 Students watch the next part of the video and make notes about the companies in the table.

Answers

	Gap	Zara
Country	USA	Spain
Where clothes are made	South-East Asia	Spain
Length of supply chain	very long	short
When it reaches the customer	eight months	four to six weeks
Types of clothing	generic looking – white T-shirts, solid colour T-shirts, jeans	fast fashion, off the catwalk – once it's gone, it's gone
Cost of production	lower	higher
How the regional capitalist economy affects their business model	It depends on where their suppliers are located and what governments enforce the activity. (liberal market economies)	It has a higher cost of production because it's making it in a higher-wage country. (coordinated market economy)

Exercise 7

Students discuss the questions in small groups.

PRE-WORK LEARNERS Ask students to work in small groups. Ask them to discuss questions 1 and 3. For question 2, ask them to think of a company they know of in their own country, or an international company, and decide how much the company relies on supply chains. If it does, how lengthy are the chains?

Exercise 8

Students answer the questions in pairs. You could remind them of the 'gig' economy from the *Talking point* in *Unit 2* (on page 21 of the *Student's Book*) and ask them what the differences between a 'sharing' economy and a 'gig' economy are. It isn't necessary to spend a long time defining the term here as they will be able to check as they watch the video.

Exercise 9

▶ **04** Give students time to read the bulleted points and then ask them to make notes on the points as they watch the video.

Exercise 10

▶ **04** Students compare the notes they made in **9** in pairs. They can then check their answers by watching the video again, and add more details.

Suggested answers

His definition of the sharing economy: taking under-utilized assets and sharing them with others

How Uber works: people employ the services of a part-time driver, who uses his/her own car, to get somewhere

How Airbnb works: people can stay in a person's home (renting a room or the whole flat/house) rather than a hotel

The positive impacts : good for consumers, generally; lower prices; quicker services

The negative impacts: creates monopoly; difficult for workers; lower wages and no benefits

Different national perspectives on the sharing economy model – US and UK preference consumer gain over anything else so it's a net winner – a very innovative model; Germany and Japan have good services that are well-regulated, and it's not necessarily all about the cheapest price but it's about giving opportunity for people to work and earn a reasonable living.

Exercise 11

In pairs, students discuss the questions. If they think there are differences between the theory and the reality, ask them to give examples.

Exercise 12

Students work in small groups. They list the positive impacts of their business on the whole community and the ways in which it is ethical.

When the group has brainstormed the list, each group presents it to the rest of the class. The class then decides if they agree on the positive impacts of the business and how ethical it is.

ONE-TO-ONE The student can watch the video and you can then answer the questions together. Have a brainstorming session together and then ask your student to write the outline based on the information and instructions in **12**.

Further ideas and video scripts

You can find a list of suggested ideas for how to use video in the class in the teacher resources in the *Online practice*. The video scripts are available to download from the Teaching Resources on the Oxford Teachers' Club. www.oup.com/elt/teacher/businessresult

Unit content

By the end of this unit, students will be able to

- discuss training
- communicate effectively on the phone and talk about the future from a past perspective
- express dissatisfaction.

Context

The topic of *Learning* will apply to your students in different ways, depending on their previous learning experiences – whether they are pre-work or in work – and if they are in work, the kind of organization they belong to. Learning was traditionally thought to end formally after school or university, but nowadays the concept of life-long learning is increasingly being embraced by both individuals and companies.

The concept of life-long learning suggests that you should always be open to new ideas, skills or behaviours, and that learning opportunities are available for all age groups. Many companies promote life-long learning through internal training and through encouraging employees to develop their skills via distance learning and postgraduate programmes. Companies who think of themselves as 'learning organizations' feel they benefit from this by increasing the level of skill within their company, and that their staff benefit as they are more likely to get promoted and are more creative and engaged in the company; sharing a corporate vision.

In this unit, students will have the opportunity to read about the concept of 'learning organizations' and then discuss their experiences of learning processes and training in their own situation. The unit then moves on to address different approaches to staff training, with a focus on effective employee development. Students will learn about effective communication strategies. They will cover talking about intentions and unfulfilled intentions. They will also have the chance to express dissatisfaction in a way that does not create communication problems. In the *Talking point* students will examine learning by sharing. They have the opportunity to come up with ideas for a 'blended-learning' programme and present these to the class.

Starting point

Students discuss the questions in pairs before comparing answers with the rest of the class. During feedback, ask students what opportunities they currently have for learning, and to what extent they use them.

Possible answers

1 Students' own answers
2 Historical events: depending on teaching methods, this is often about learning facts and figures. They can be memorized, and are not necessarily learnt within any meaningful context.
How to cook: this is likely to be 'learning by doing', making mistakes and getting better results each time.
How to negotiate: there are certain strategies that can be followed and learnt. Some people are natural negotiators, while others find it much more difficult.
How to balance work and private life: something many people, however long they have worked, find very difficult. Time-management courses can help people learn to prioritize their tasks.
3 Students' own answers

PRE-WORK LEARNERS For question 3, ask students to think about courses they have done in the past, for example, first aid courses, cookery courses, summer/winter sports courses. In small groups, ask them to discuss what was good about the course they did, and what they thought was less useful or successful about the course. They can decide if they think they learnt anything on the course and if so, what? They can also say whether or not they recommend the course they did to a friend, and why/why not.

Working with words

Exercise 1

Ask students what the terms 'learning organization' and 'systems thinking' might mean. Write their ideas on the board. Then ask them to read the text and compare their ideas. Before they read, you might want to check that students understand the following:

nurture = to help somebody/something to develop and become successful

Answers

learning organization: an organization that can get the results it really wants by encouraging and enabling employees to achieve those goals in any way they choose
systems thinking: being able to see the organization as a whole

Exercise 2

Students read the text again and answer questions 1–2 in pairs. Before they read, you might want to check that students understand the following:

upheaval = a big change that causes a lot of confusion, worry, and problems

deferential = showing that you respect someone/something

Answers

1 Getting greater commitment and involvement from employees and encouraging creativity could lead to more innovation and, ultimately, better results for a company. The focus on staff development could also mean that staff are less likely to leave, so teams will be stronger and recruitment costs lower.

2 For: usually leads to improved results; all staff are encouraged to be creative and take a holistic view of the business
Against: can cause structural upheaval; requires a major change in thinking; the changes required may be unrealistic; it may be more difficult to organize training for staff as a whole, rather than the individual; management may still continue to impose values from the top; the workforce may still end up having to 'look up' to top management; individuals don't necessarily need to be involved in and aware of the overall running of the business, but should focus on their own work/contribution to the business

Exercise 3

Students match the phrases in bold in the text in **1** to definitions 1–8.

Answers

1 personal development plan
2 skills deficit
3 shared vision
4 performance management
5 employee participation
6 paradigm shift
7 structural change
8 collective aspiration

Exercise 4

Students complete the sentences with the underlined phrases from the text in **1**.

Answers

1 in the real world
2 the bigger picture
3 across the board
4 in the long-run

EXTRA ACTIVITY

Draw the table below on the board. Only write the words in bold (words from the text). Ask students to work in pairs and complete the table in their notebooks. They should also underline the stressed syllables (see underlined sections in the table). Check their answers as a class. You could also ask students to rewrite sentences from the texts that include the words in bold, using a different form of the word.

Answers

NOUN (thing)	NOUN (person)	VERB	ADJECTIVE
organization	organizer	organize	organizational
expanse	–		expansive
capacity	–	be capable of	capable
creation	creator	create	creative
desire	–	desire	desirable
aspiration	–	aspire to	aspirational
system	–	systematize	systematic
emphasis	–	emphasize	emphatic
practice	practitioner	practise	practical
suggestion	–	suggest	suggested
encouragement	–	encourage	encouraging
success	successor	succeed	successful
reality	realist	realize	realistic
suspicion	suspect	suspect	suspicious
participation	participant	participate	participative
imposition	impostor	impose	imposing

Exercise 5

Students work in pairs and discuss what advice they would give in each situation. Encourage them to use the vocabulary from **3** and **4** and the phrases from the list.

Possible answers

1 *They should* have individual personal development plans.
2 *There needs to be* a shared vision so that all employees are aware of the bigger picture.
3 *There needs to be* a structural change in the company.
4 *There's a lack of* skills across the board.
5 *There isn't any* employee participation.

Exercise 6

▶ **7.1** Students listen and answer the questions. They can then compare their answers with a partner. Before they listen, you might want to check that students understand the following:

remit = the area of activity over which a particular person or group has authority, control or influence

trigger = to make something happen or cause a reaction

Answers
1 Yes, to some extent, because they try to get employees thinking about the implications of their work in a larger context, rather than just the job itself.
2 job-specific training and generic training
3 Advantages: It can be quite responsive to employees' needs; they can provide a variety of training opportunities; training is more self-directed; staff take ownership of their learning and are therefore more committed.
Disadvantages: A lot of different courses need to be run to cater to individual needs, which means that resources are not always used very efficiently.

Exercise 7

▶ **7.1** Write the words *training* and *approach* on the board and elicit examples of adjectives that collocate with each, e.g. *job-specific training, bottom-up approach*. Students then listen again and make a note of the adjectives used.

Answers
1 job-specific training, generic training, centrally-driven training, self-directed training
2 bottom-up approach, decentralized approach, top-down approach, one-size-fits-all approach

Exercise 8

Students match the adjectives from **7** to the definitions 1–5.

Answers
1 generic/one-size-fits-all
2 centrally-driven/top-down
3 bottom-up/decentralized
4 job-specific
5 self-directed

Further practice

If students need more practice, go to *Practice file 7* on page 114 of the *Student's Book*.

Exercise 9

Students work in pairs and turn to page 140 of the *Student's Book* and read the information. They can then discuss the answers. Encourage them to use vocabulary from this section where appropriate.

Possible answers
Company 1 could be seen to have a responsive approach to training, with each department deciding what it needs. In a small company this could work well as it responds quickly to need and employees can have contact in other ways. However, in a large company, it might be difficult to create a company ethos as training for different departments could have different aims and outcomes. If the training comes from many different sources, there could also be a problem with quality control. Without any in-house training, there is no opportunity for the employees to work with people from other departments and gain an insight as to how the whole company works. There is normally a bottom-up approach but individual employees having to ask for the money for training could place new employees who would potentially benefit more from training at a disadvantage.

Company 2 has a top-down approach but gives a lot of opportunity for training. It is useful for the company to have a formalized approach to create a company approach. If the manager decides on the training, this could benefit the company by making sure the team has all the requisite skills. However, while the idea of having to complete two courses in the first year or two of a new job is reasonably attractive, the idea that an employee has to complete two courses every year after that seems like overkill; almost a 'ticking the box' approach.

Exercise 10

If possible, students from the same company should work together to discuss their ideas. Monitor for correct use of the vocabulary from **3**, **4** and **8**. Give feedback after the activity.

ALTERNATIVE If you have students from different companies, ask them to note down their ideas and answers, and then compare them with someone from a different company. Write the following questions on the board to guide their discussion:

• *Which approach do you think is best, and why?*
• *Would you like to work in your partner's company? Why/Why not?*

PRE-WORK LEARNERS If students have worked for an organization part-time, or on a temporary basis, they could refer to that experience. Otherwise, ask them to decide what sort of company they would like to work in, and how they would like their training to be organized.

Photocopiable worksheet

Download and photocopy *Unit 7 Working with words worksheet* from the teacher resources in the *Online practice*.

Business communication

Exercise 1

▶ **7.2–7.3** Ask students to read the *Context* and brainstorm what decisions Kirsten would have to make when planning next year's training programme, e.g. details of training courses, names of relevant staff, dates for courses, who the training providers will be, face-to-face or distance learning, costs, etc. Students then listen and answer the question.

Answers
The main problem is that Kirsten thinks they don't have the expertise to run the training courses required. The eventual solution is that they decide to use outside trainers.

Exercise 2

▶ **7.2–7.3** Students listen again and complete the expressions.

Answers
1 you say
2 clear about your last suggestion
3 run it by me
4 you're saying
5 not that
6 clarify exactly
7 their name
8 did you
9 to spell out
10 I'm saying is
11 mean that
12 quite sure
13 What I mean

Exercise 3

Students match the expressions in **2** to categories a–f. They can then check their answers in pairs.

Answers
a 1, 7, 8
b 2, 12
c 3
d 4, 11
e 6, 9
f 5, 10, 13

EXTENSION Write the following sentences on the board. Ask students to identify the repetition in each example (see words in bold).

*It's not that **we don't have the** trainers. **We don't have the** expertise.*

*That wasn't quite **what I meant to say**. **What I meant to say** was that we'll have to run this internally after all.*

Ask students why repetition is used in these examples (to help the speaker communicate their point clearly and powerfully). Then write the following situation on the board and elicit a conversation from students, including repetition.

Situation: Idea for new product.

A *Thinks B doesn't like it.*

B *Likes the idea, but a competitor has already done it.*

Suggested answer
A So, you don't like the idea?
B It's not **what I meant. What I meant** was that the idea itself is good, but it's already been done by the competition.

Exercise 4

▶ **7.4** Students correct the mistakes. They then listen to check their answers. You could ask students to mark the stress on the correct words and expressions (see underlining below).

Answers
1 ~~relative~~ <u>r</u>elevant
2 ~~outside the topic~~ <u>off</u>-topic
3 ~~recalls~~ re<u>minds</u>
4 ~~digress~~ di<u>gression</u>
5 ~~at~~ to
6 ~~this way~~ the <u>way</u>

Exercise 5

Students focus on the corrected expressions in **4** and answer the questions.

Answers
a 1, 3, 6
b 2, 4, 5

Further practice
If students need more practice, go to *Practice file 7* on page 115 of the *Student's Book*.

Exercise 6

Students choose a topic individually and make notes on it.

PRE-WORK LEARNERS Write the topics below on the board and ask students to choose one they find interesting. Ask them to make notes of some true things they can say about it.

1 *The next stage of your studies or what you intend to do after your studies*

2 *A difficulty you have encountered in your studies, which you find hard to cope with*

3 *Something you find irritating about your college and would like to change*

4 *A suggestion you have for improving your way of studying*

Exercise 7

Students work in pairs and have a phone call using the topic they chose in **6**. They should follow the flow chart. Encourage them to use language from the *Key expressions*.

ALTERNATIVE Ask students to work in groups of three. Two students have the phone call whilst the third student listens and ticks (✓) any language in the *Key expressions* that they use. They should also note any mistakes. They can then give feedback to the other students before changing roles and repeating the process.

> **CULTURE QUESTION**
> Ask students to discuss the questions in groups. Make sure they consider both business contexts and those with friends and family. You might want to discuss attitudes towards personal space. This tends to differ according to culture. In Latin cultures, people are more likely to tolerate relatively small amounts of personal space, whereas in Northern cultures it is likely to be bigger. Lack of awareness of these different preferences could cause misunderstandings. Warn students not to be too influenced by stereotypes as these are generalizations.

Photocopiable worksheet

Download and photocopy *Unit 7 Business communication worksheet* from the teacher resources in the *Online practice*.

Language at work

Exercise 1

Students look at the extract from the conversation between Tamara and Kirsten and answer questions 1–4.

Answers
1 make an excuse
2 no
3 sometime before 'this morning'
4 It describes a situation which was a future situation at a given point in the past, but it didn't actually take place.

Exercise 2

Students match the examples a–g to the things they express 1–7.

Answers
1 c   2 a   3 g   4 b   5 d   6 e   7 f

Grammar reference

If students need more information, go to *Grammar Reference* on page 130 of the *Student's Book*.

Exercise 3

Students work with a partner and decide what the speaker could say in situations 1–5.

Possible answers
2 I was planning/going to go to Moscow next week to a conference, but my boss has decided I should go to New York instead.
3 We thought / We had hoped / We were hoping we'd make a profit this year, but unfortunately …
4 We were aiming to get a 10% discount, but now they're telling us …
5 I was having / I was going to have / I was going to be having / I had planned to have lunch with Maria tomorrow, but she has cancelled because …

EXTRA ACTIVITY

Ask students to look at the tenses that are used in the sentences in **3**. What would the speaker have said when the plans were still OK? Write the first one on the board and discuss it as a class.

*I was **going to bring** a sample of the new product with me.*
***I'm bringing** a sample of the new product to the meeting.*

Answers
2 I'm planning to go / I'm going to be going to Moscow next week / I'm going to Moscow next week.
3 We're bound to make a profit. / We'll definitely make a profit.
4 We are aiming to get a 10% discount.
5 I'm having lunch with Maria tomorrow.

Further practice

If students need more practice, go to *Practice file 7* on page 115 of the *Student's Book*.

Exercise 4

Students read the situations and think of their own examples. Allow time for them to make notes on what happened. They then take turns to explain to their partner what happened, using the 'future in the past' where appropriate. You can then ask students to describe their experiences to the rest of the class. Encourage the other students to ask questions to find out more.

Monitor for correct use of the 'future in the past'. After the activity, write any incorrect sentences on the board and ask the class to correct the mistakes

PRE-WORK LEARNERS Ask students to choose similar situations, but related to their studies, or private life.

ALTERNATIVE Ask students to write down some past intentions they had, but which didn't happen as planned (see the examples below). They can then share their experiences in pairs.

- I was going to give up smoking, but faced with the prospect of working on a stressful project without cigarettes, I decided not to.
- After my last course finished, I was going to do 30 minutes of English homework a day, but given the fact that I had to do overtime I just didn't have time.
- I had intended to tidy my desk at the end of each day, but having realized how untidy I am by nature I didn't keep it up.

Photocopiable worksheet

Download and photocopy *Unit 7 Language at work worksheet* from the teacher resources in the *Online practice*.

Practically speaking

Exercise 1

▶ **7.5** As a lead-in, ask students to think about a time when they weren't satisfied with something (e.g. at a meeting, on holiday, etc.). Then ask students to describe exactly why they weren't satisfied to the rest of the class. Elicit possible phrases students could have used to express their dissatisfaction. Students then listen and answer the questions.

Answers
1
Conversation 1: in a coffee break, probably at a training session
Conversation 2: in an office / at work, discussing designs for a brochure
Conversation 3: in a meeting
2
Conversation 1: The first speaker feels they haven't learnt anything, but the second speaker is a little less critical.
Conversation 2: The second speaker doesn't find the design or wording suitable.
Conversation 3: The second speaker doesn't feel the next topic is relevant to him, and therefore feels he cannot contribute.
3
Conversation 1: Similar, although the second speaker is more optimistic.
Conversation 2: The second speaker is quite critical and because the first speaker accepts the criticism, they make a suggestion to help the situation.
Conversation 3: no

Exercise 2

▶ **7.5** Students complete extracts 1–11 from the conversations in **1** and then listen again to check their answers.

Answers
1 much out of
2 doing my head in
3 testing my patience
4 reached my limit
5 lived up to expectations
6 was expecting something a bit more
7 it's just not up to scratch
8 not very happy with
9 can't really see the point of
10 finding it a bit frustrating
11 don't think this is the best use of

Exercise 3

Students match sentences 1–11 in **2** to categories a–e. They can then check their answers in pairs.

Answers
a 7, 8
b 5, 6
c 1, 9, 11
d 2, 3, 10
e 4

Exercise 4

Students underline the words the speaker uses to soften what they say.

You may need to mention that in the UK people can *seem* to be less direct/forceful because they use these softeners. However, it doesn't mean the person is less dissatisfied, it is simply the way people express their dissatisfaction. It is important that students recognize when British people are expressing real dissatisfaction when doing business. This is not the case in the USA where people are generally more direct.

Answers
1 to be honest, I think, a bit of
2 really
3 I have to admit, really
4 I'm afraid, some

EXTENSION Write the following sentences on the board and ask students how they could be made less direct. Add their ideas to the board.

1 *This report is terrible.*
2 *The talk was really boring.*
3 *Your report is far too long.*
4 *I hope you'll change your mind.*

Then ask students to look at their ideas on the board and identify which of the following methods they used to make the sentences less direct.

• using a softening phrase (e.g. *I'm afraid, to be honest*)

• using positive adjectives/verbs with *not,* rather than negative ones (e.g. *not enjoying* instead of *hate*; *not (very) interesting* instead of *boring*)

• making things sound 'smaller' by adding *some, really, rather, a bit,* etc.

Possible answers
1 (using a softening phrase) I'm afraid I think the report is unsatisfactory. / To be honest, I was expecting something rather more informative.
2 (using positive verbs with *not*) I can't say I enjoyed the talk. (making things sound 'smaller' by adding *a bit*): It was a bit difficult to sit through.
3 (using positive adjectives with *not*) I didn't find the report very useful. It wasn't very precise.
(making things sound 'smaller' by adding *rather*) It was rather lengthy / over-long.
4 (using a softening phrase) To be honest, I'm not sure you're making the right decision.

Exercise 5

Students work in pairs to soften sentences 1–5.

Possible answers
1 I'm afraid your performance this year has been somewhat/a bit below standard.
2 I have to admit that I'm not really enjoying the project I'm working on at the moment.
3 I'm sorry to tell you, but you need to rewrite rather a lot of your presentation.
4 I have to say that I feel that this meeting isn't hugely productive.
5 I'd like to know what the purpose is of our being here. There doesn't seem to be very much to do.

Useful phrases
Refer students to the *Useful phrases* section on page 135 of the *Student's Book* for extension and revision.

Exercise 6

Students read the situations and work in pairs to decide what phrases from **2** could be used. They then have the conversations. Monitor and make notes of particularly good uses of softening phrases for the feedback stage.

Ask students to look again at the situations in **6**. Then write the following questions on the board:

1 *What would you say in these situations if you were talking to:*

   a your boss

   b an important visitor to your company?

2 *Is the language very different from what you would use with colleagues? If so, how?*

Possible answers

Situation 1 (bad coffee in the coffee machine)

To your boss: *I think the coffee cold be improved.*

To an important visitor to your company: *I'm afraid I don't usually drink this coffee. I prefer to make my own.*

The language used with the boss is likely to be less critical than the language used with a colleague. The language used with the visitor enables the speaker to hide what they really think – there is no open criticism and the visitor is left to deduce for themselves why the person doesn't drink the coffee at work.

Situation 2 (long presentation)

To your boss: *Perhaps the presentation could have been a bit more succinct.*

To an important visitor to your company: *The presentation could have been slimmed down a little, don't you think?*

The language to your boss is tentative (use of modal *could*) and to the visitor is rather impersonal.

Situation 3 (low bonus)

To your boss: *The bonus is rather disappointing this year.*

To an important visitor: You would not discuss payments with him/her.

Situation 4 (irrelevant presentation)

To your boss: *I'll go if you think I should, but I'm really worried that I won't be able to make the deadline for the present project. We have a very tight schedule.*

To an important visitor: *There's a really interesting presentation this morning on … I'll take you to the room so you can hear it, but I'm afraid I have to meet a deadline today, so I won't be able to stay and listen.*

When making excuses we tend to make longer sentences with more softening vocabulary.

Students match the phrases with *say* to the meanings.

Answers

1 e 2 f 3 b 4 c 5 a 6 d

Talking point

Discussion

Exercise 1

Students read the article and answer the question. They can compare answers with a partner. Allow a few minutes for students to read the *Context* and the article. Be prepared to answer any questions about vocabulary.

Answer

Hyla thinks support from supervisors and use of shared experiences are lacking in the corporate learning and training process.

Exercise 2

Students compare the different kinds of 'learning interventions' in the article and discuss their answer with a partner.

Exercise 3

Students work in pairs or small groups and describe the training in their company.

PRE-WORK LEARNERS Ask students to work in groups and decide which of the 'learning interventions' they think would be the most successful and to give reasons. Which would they most like to find in a company they started to work for? You could ask them to pick a company and find out what its training approach is from its website to follow up.

Task

Exercise 1

Students work with a partner. They read the list of training methods and decide which ones to use for new employees. If they work for the same company, they can state which would work best in that company. If they work for different companies, they can decide on one company or make up an imaginary one and make the best choices for that.

Allow pairs time to prepare their presentations. Remind them to include the points given and add any extra ideas they have. They should be ready to give reasons for their choices and explain the advantages for employees and the company. They should also be prepared to answer questions about the presentation.

PRE-WORK LEARNERS Students read the list of training methods. They can then decide what sort of company they work for and decide which methods to use in a blended-learning programme for new employees. They then prepare and give a presentation following the points in **1**, explaining the reasons for their choice and the advantages for the company and the employees.

Exercise 2

Pairs now present their plans to another group. You could encourage the students who are listening to write down any questions they have during the presentation and ask them at the end.

You could also ask students to decide as a class which training methods are the most popular and the reasons for their popularity. The class could come up with a class list of methods.

Give feedback on the use of language. Write any mistakes on the board and ask the class to correct them.

ONE-TO-ONE The student can read the *Context* and the article and answer the questions. Ask him/her to read the list of training methods and decide which ones to use for new employees in their company. Ask him/her to give a presentation of their plan and be ready to answer questions on it. As you listen, write down three or four questions about the plan for the student to answer.

| Progress test

Download and photocopy *Unit 7 Progress test* and *Speaking test* from the teacher resources in the *Online practice*.

Unit content

By the end of this unit, students will be able to
- discuss performance at work
- give informal presentations and deal with questions.

Context

Performance in business is not only important for companies – it's also an essential part of an employee's career development. If employee performance is evaluated and enhanced through training and support, an individual is likely to be more motivated and driven. This will in turn be of benefit to the company itself.

Companies now recognize that improving employee satisfaction will enable them to retain their staff and improve performance across the board. Research has suggested that financial compensation is in fact relatively low on an employee's list of priorities and that more important issues include recognition, good teams and teamwork, having a sense of loyalty to the company, and being able to make a positive contribution to the company.

This unit approaches the topic of performance from two angles of employer–employee expectations. Firstly, the issues of employee motivation and happiness are considered and students have the opportunity to discuss how this may affect the performance of an individual. Students then listen to what employers want from employees and they work out what an ideal employee might be. The focus then turns towards staff performance in business situations and in particular during impromptu presentations. Students have the chance to practise giving presentations under pressure with little or no preparation, going through the stages that help make a presentation clear and memorable. They then focus on using questions in an impromptu presentation situation, and how to deal with challenging questions. The *Talking point* examines performance reviews and new thinking on the process. Students have the opportunity to draw up performance measures for jobs in a company.

Starting point

Discuss the questions as a class. Note any ideas on the board. You could then ask students to tell you about any rewards or forms of recognition in their companies.

Possible answers
1 know-how from other companies in the industry; expertise in particular skills; specialist knowledge; language skills; enthusiasm; connections with important people in a field, etc.
2 being paid on commission; bonuses; a company car; the chance to work on another project; an opportunity to train further; promotion; staff parties, etc.

Working with words

Exercise 1

Students make a list. They can then discuss and compare their ideas in small groups.

PRE-WORK LEARNERS Ask students to think about how working will be different from studying. Write the following question on the board for discussion:

What do you expect will help you enjoy working for a company in the future?

Possible answers
working with good people / teamwork; recognition for good work / being rewarded; being independent and allowed to take decisions; getting support from colleagues; being challenged; being paid well; having flexible working times; driving a company car, etc.

Exercise 2

Students read the text and compare their ideas in **1**.

Answers
feeling part of a friendly and supporting atmosphere; having a say in what happens; enjoying 'a fun workspace'; enjoyable work; gaining satisfaction from achievements; being able to relate to the values of the company; making a worthwhile contribution to the company; doing something good for the environment

Exercise 3

Students complete phrases 1–6 with a noun from the text in **2**. They can then check their answers by referring to the text.

Answers
1 difference
2 recognition
3 part
4 say
5 pride
6 future

DICTIONARY SKILLS

Ask students to work in pairs and to look up two words in **3** in a monolingual dictionary. Ask them to find other phrases and collocations using these words. They should note them down, along with the meaning.

For example:

difference

a marked difference = a strong difference

tell the difference (between) = distinguish

a world of difference = very different

have our differences = to have disagreements

settle one's differences = to resolve disagreements

Then ask pairs to write example sentences for each phrase/collocation.

Exercise 4

Students match the phrases in **3** to definitions a–f.

Answers
a 2 **b** 4 **c** 5 **d** 1 **e** 3 **f** 6

EXTENSION Ask students to close their books. Write the following phrases on the board and ask students to tell you which preposition should follow each one (answers are in brackets).

1 *make a difference (to)*

2 *gain recognition (for)*

3 *have a say (in)*

4 *take pride (in)*

5 *feel part (of)*

6 *see a future (for)*

Then ask students to write their own example sentence for each phrase.

Exercise 5

Students work in pairs and discuss how satisfied they are at work, using phrases from **3**.

PRE-WORK LEARNERS Write the following questions on the board and ask students to discuss them in pairs:

• *Do you take pride in the assignments you hand in? Why/Why not?*

• *Do you think you would make a difference to a team you were part of? In what ways would you bring something to a team?*

Exercise 6

▶ **8.1–8.2** Students listen and match the conversations with the pictures, then answer the questions. Before they listen, you might want to check that students understand the following:

prospective = expected, future

lateral moves = sideways moves to other departments, rather than further up in the same department

strive = to make an effort

Answers
1 Company 1: De Beers = looks for people with qualities of leadership, accountability, collaboration and passion.
Company 2: Credit Suisse = looks for people with a combination of specialist know-how and personality, committed to individual achievement, with a strong team spirit, and who are able to build rapport and credibility easily.
2 Students' own answers

Exercise 7

▶ **8.1–8.2** Students complete the phrases with a preposition. They can then compare their ideas in pairs before listening again to check their answers.

Answers

1	of	**7**	to
2	in	**8**	with
3	into	**9**	to
4	of	**10**	for
5	up	**11**	up, with
6	in	**12**	for

Further practice

If students need more practice, go to *Practice file 8* on page 116 of the *Student's Book*.

Exercise 8

Students think of examples from their own experience and then discuss them in pairs. Encourage them to use at least four of the phrases from **7**.

PRE-WORK LEARNERS Ask students to talk about experiences they have had during their studies, whilst working part-time, or in their personal life.

Exercise 9

Students can focus on their own company, or they can choose one of the company profiles on page 141 of the *Student's Book* to work with. Students work in two groups. Ask each group to brainstorm ideas relating to their expectations.

ONE-TO-ONE Ask the student to think about his/her own company. Ask him/her to prepare some notes on the following questions and present them to you.

• What does he/she consider the qualities of an ideal employee are from the employer's point of view?

• What can a company do to attract and keep the ideal employee?

• What can the company expect in return for this?

Exercise 10

Students now pair up with someone from the other group. They should imagine they are at a careers fair. They have an informal discussion and then decide how well-suited they are to each other. Monitor the use of the vocabulary from this section.

At the end of the activity, ask students which pairs were most well-suited to each other and why. Give positive feedback to students who used vocabulary from **3** and **7** effectively.

ONE-TO-ONE Ask the student to imagine he/she is at a careers fair for young graduates/school-leavers. Discuss the following questions:

- How would he/she attract a young person to the company?
- What would he/she want the young person to offer as a potential employee?
- Does the student have any experience of employing people? What are the main points to think about when looking for new employees?

Photocopiable worksheet

Download and photocopy *Unit 8 Working with words worksheet* from the teacher resources in the *Online practice*.

Business communication

Exercise 1

Ask students to work in pairs and discuss the questions.

Answers

1 An impromptu presentation is one where there has been little or no advance preparation – someone may have asked you to give a short talk without any warning. This is particularly common in team meetings. Due to the lack of preparation, there won't usually be any visuals or handouts to support the presentation. The audience is likely to be smaller and the content will be less structured. There will be a lot of redundancy (*um, er*, repetition, etc.) and the aim is more likely to be related to informing or explaining, rather than being persuasive.
2 Students' own answers

EXTRA ACTIVITY

Write some simple topics on pieces of paper, and fold them in half. Topics could include: *My favourite restaurant; My plans for the future; My next holiday; Why I applied to work for this company; A recent business trip; A conference / training course I attended recently; A terrible day I had at work/college*, etc. There should be one topic per student.

In turn, ask each student to take a piece of paper and give a two-minute talk on the topic (without any preparation). Discourage the others from interrupting during the talk. When they have all finished, ask students which talk they liked best, and why. Then find out how difficult it was, and what made it easy or difficult.

Exercise 2

▶ **8.3–8.4** Ask students to read the *Context* about Ovanta. Ask students who Anya and Pavla are and why they are making an impromptu presentation at the meeting. (Anya is in charge of a research project into the company's training needs, and Pavla is working on improving industrial relations. Neither has been asked to give a formal presentation but has been invited to the meeting to brief senior management.) Students then listen to extracts 1 and 2 and answer the questions. They can then check their answers in pairs before comparing answers with the rest of the class.

Answers

1 b 2 a 3 b 4 a 5 b

Exercise 3

▶ **8.3** Students listen again to extract 1 and complete the sentences.

Answers

1 Where we are at the moment is
2 what I can tell you is that
3 I'd like to be able to, but unfortunately I can't
4 You'll appreciate that I still need to
5 perhaps it would be a good idea if I just
6 I'd just like to sketch out
7 Let me just touch on
8 I think that's covered everything

Exercise 4

Students match the expressions in **3** to the categories.

Answers

a expressions 5–8
b expressions 1–4

Exercise 5

Students are going to take part in a meeting. To build up to it, they work on the language for each stage. This first stage is the context. Ask students to work in pairs. Allow time for them to read the information. They then discuss what they could say to set the context and signal key points.

Possible answers

a I'd like to be able to hand over the full report now, but unfortunately I can't because we're still waiting for all the questionnaires to come back in.
  Where we are at the moment is that we're still processing the feedback.
  Let me just touch on the issue of 'effective questionnaires'.
b Perhaps it would be a good idea if I explained some of the difficulties we've had.
  I'd just like to sketch out the general findings from the responses we've received so far.

Exercise 6

Students work in pairs and brainstorm possible expressions for highlighting the main points in an impromptu presentation they have to give. They then turn to audio script 8.4 on page 154 and compare their ideas with the expressions used.

Answers

So, the first thing is …
And I think you should be aware that …
So that's one key point right there.
… and I think this is a really important point …
So, the main thing to remember is …

Exercise 7

▶ **8.3–8.4** Students listen again and note down the responses to the questions.

Answers
1 I was coming to that. It's obviously a key area, and I have to admit that we haven't got as far as planning the specifics yet – we just haven't had the time.
2 That's a good point. I think so. Let me check, and I'll get back to you.
3 I can't remember exactly, but … off the top of my head, I think everyone had something to say. That's quite a significant factor, though … I can double check if you like?
4 Well, I don't have the exact figures, but what if I run through the rough numbers we've come up with so far?

Further practice

If students need more practice, go to *Practice file 8* on page 116 of the *Student's Book*.

Exercise 8

Students work in pairs and take turns to respond to the questions.

Possible answers
1 I have to admit, it has taken longer than expected.
2 I was coming to that. I don't have the schedule with me, but I think it's achievable in the time frame. Let me check after the meeting and I'll get back to you.
3 I was coming to that. We avoided any leading questions and most of them were multiple-choice.
4 I can't remember exactly, but off the top of my head I think it was 150.
5 That's a good point. However, I think the data will still be relevant. People don't tend to change their views on these issues overnight.
6 I was coming to that. Yes, we've already started planning the next research project. I don't have the exact details with me, but what if I asked Janice to email the initial plan to you after the meeting?

Exercise 9

Students work in small groups. They are going to take part in the meeting and use all the language they have practised in **5–8**. Allow time for them to think of their projects and to prepare the agenda. They should then take turns to give impromptu presentations.

Monitor for good use of the expressions in the *Key expressions* and give feedback on this.

PRE-WORK LEARNERS Ask students to think of current study projects they are working on or any leisure activities they are involved in.

ONE-TO-ONE Ask the student to think about his/her own company. Ask him/her to think of a new product or service his/her company might develop. Ask them to make notes in order to brief you about it. Remind them to use the *Key expressions* to set the context, signal his/her intention during the presentation, and highlight the key points. While you listen to the presentation, be sure to ask questions to get the student to respond to questions, challenges and requests for detail.

EXTENSION If possible, record the impromptu presentations to allow you to analyse students' fluency and use of language. In the next lesson, play each recording and ask students to note down any fillers used (small words and sounds used while a speaker is thinking, e.g. *um, er, like, you know,* etc.). It's often useful for students to hear themselves speaking and to see whether they are using one particular filler too often, as this will impede their level of fluency.

When students have a list of fillers, they should match them to the following functions:
1 giving yourself thinking time
2 clarifying what you have said
3 giving an example
4 other

Then ask them to think of possible alternative fillers for each category. Encourage them to try incorporating these alternative fillers into their language to improve their level of fluency. For example:
1 Let me just think … / I'm sure you know, … / So perhaps I'll just …
2 What I mean is … / What I'm trying to say is … / Let me put it another way, …
3 So for example, … / Let me give you an example. / So, for instance, …

Photocopiable worksheet

Download and photocopy *Unit 8 Business communication worksheet* from the teacher resources in the *Online practice*.

Language at work

Exercise 1

Students match the questions to the categories (more than one match may be possible). They can then compare their answers in pairs before comparing answers with the rest of the class.

Answers
a 1, 9
b 2, 4, 7
c 3, 8, 10
d 5, 6

Exercise 2

Students categorize the questions in **1**. More than one category is possible for some questions.

Answers
a 1, 2, 9
b 4, 6, 7
c 4, 5, 6, 7, 10
d 3, 8
e 1, 6
f 4, 5, 7
g 2, 3, 8, 9, 10

Grammar reference

If students need more information, go to *Grammar reference* on page 130 of the *Student's Book*.

Exercise 3

Students work in pairs and take turns to ask questions. Encourage them to refer back to the question types in **1** to help them.

> **Possible answers**
> 1 Do you really think that is a good idea?
> 2 Phil, you've got the latest figures – would you mind talking us through them?
> 3 I assume you've all had a chance to look at the draft, have you?
> 4 Now, how can I put this …?
> 5 I don't know if you're familiar with the new software?
> 6 Do you think it was wise to show the findings to the client before checking with the boss?
> 7 I take it the research phase has been completed, has it?
> 8 Bob, can you give us an overview of your research trip?

EXTENSION Ask students to work in pairs. Each student should write eight questions that they would like to ask their partner, using various question types. They then take turns to ask and answer questions.

Further practice

If students need more practice, go to *Practice file 8* on page 117 of the *Student's Book*.

Exercise 4

Students work in groups of three. Each student should prepare some information about a recent project, making a few bullet points on paper (not full sentences). Give them about two minutes. When they are ready, Students A and B should start. Student C should take notes, writing down each question, who says it, and the function of the question. When they have finished, they should change roles and repeat.

Ask students to give their feedback on the questions that were used in their groups. How many questions were asked? How many different functions were used? Were the questions suitably varied? Were the responses appropriate?

PRE-WORK LEARNERS Students should focus on a study project or another kind of project that they are working on.

ONE-TO-ONE Ask the student to think about his/her work over the past couple of weeks and make a few notes on the main points. Then tell him/her that you are their line manager and that you want an update on his/her work over the past couple of weeks. Interrupt as often as you can with a variety of questions. If necessary, ask the student to move on and talk about a new point.

Photocopiable worksheet

Download and photocopy *Unit 8 Language at work worksheet* from the teacher resources in the *Online practice*.

Practically speaking

Exercise 1

As a lead-in, ask students why some questions are difficult to answer.

> **Possible answers**
> because you don't know the answer
> because the truthful answer may be unpopular
> because the truthful answer may give others a bad impression of you
> because you hadn't anticipated the question, so you hadn't thought about an answer

Students then discuss the questions in pairs.

> **Possible answers**
> 1 explain that you don't want to answer; try to delay giving an answer; give some possibly false information; admit that you don't know the answer
> 2 pretend that you don't know the answer; admit that you don't want to answer; refer the person to someone else

Exercise 2

▶ **8.5** Students listen to six conversations and tick (✓) the strategies used to respond to the questions.

> **Answers**
>
> | Strategies | 1 | 2 | 3 | 4 | 5 | 6 |
> |---|---|---|---|---|---|---|
> | admit ignorance | | ✓ | ✓ | ✓ | | |
> | directly refuse to answer | ✓ | ✓ | | | | ✓ |
> | avoid the question | | | | ✓ | ✓ | ✓ |
> | distance yourself from the situation | ✓ | | ✓ | | ✓ | |

Exercise 3

▶ **8.5** Students listen again and note down phrases the speakers used for the strategies in **2**. They can then compare their answers in pairs before comparing answers with the rest of the class.

> **Answers**
> Admit ignorance: I'm afraid I don't know any more than you do. / Sorry, I don't know what you mean. / I'm afraid I'm not up to speed on …
> Directly refuse to answer: I'm sorry, but I can't answer that. / I would prefer not to talk about it. / I'm afraid I can't disclose that information – it's confidential.
> Avoid the question: Well, it's not that straightforward. / It's hard to say at the moment. / I can't really comment.
> Distance yourself from the situation: I'm afraid I'm really not in a position to talk about that. / It's not for me to say. / It's nothing to do with me.

Write the following questions on the board. Ask students to discuss them in pairs, before comparing answers with the rest of the class.

1 *Have you ever been asked a difficult question …?*
  - *in a job interview*
  - *during a speaking exam*
  - *in a meeting*
  - *during a product presentation*
  - *by your boss*
  - *in front of your mother*
  - *at a formal dinner*
  - *in an appraisal*

  If so, what was the question? Did you deal with it well or badly? Why?

2 *Which jobs demand an ability to deal with difficult questions well?* (Possible answers could include politicians, PR representatives, CEOs, teachers, etc.)

3 *Can you think of any examples of someone in the public eye who deals particularly well or badly with questions? Who?*

Useful phrases

Refer students to the *Useful phrases* section on page 135 of the *Student's Book* for extension and revision.

Exercise 4

Students work in pairs. Student A reads the information on page 67 of the *Student's Book* and Student B turns to page 141. Allow time for them to read their information and to think about what questions they can ask and how they'll answer their partner's questions. They should then take turns to ask questions and respond.

Exercise 5

Students might like to swap pairs for this activity. Allow time for students to write two difficult questions. They then take turns to ask and answer. Monitor and make a note of the phrases they use for asking and responding.

When they have finished, ask them if they were able to ask appropriate and difficult questions. Were they able to answer the questions? Then give feedback on their use of language. Write any errors on the board for the class to correct.

PRE-WORK LEARNERS Ask students to choose a topic they'd be willing to discuss, e.g. their course, an exam, their plans after their studies, etc.

CULTURE QUESTION

Ask students to discuss these questions in small groups. If they need help with the second question, suggest the following phrases:

I'd rather not answer that, if you don't mind. / Actually, I'd prefer not to answer that.

This is usually suitable and effective in Western Europe.

KEY WORD

Students match the use of *just* to the definitions.

Answers
1 c 2 a 3 d 4 e 5 b

Progress test

Download and photocopy *Unit 8 Progress test* and *Speaking test* from the teacher resources in the *Online practice*.

Talking point

Discussion

Exercise 1

Allow a few minutes for students to read the *Context* and the article and be prepared to answer any questions about vocabulary.

Students answer the questions from their own experience.

PRE-WORK LEARNERS Ask students to think about occasions they have had feedback and/or tutorials from teachers/ lecturers. What did they find most useful? What did they find least useful?

Exercise 2

Tell students to make a list of pros and cons under each of the headings: the company; the manager; the employee. Then students can work in pairs or small groups and discuss their ideas.

Possible answers

Pros: It allows for a more instantaneous and timely feedback system. It means that employees can feel they are appreciated at the time, they do not need to push themselves once a year. Timely feedback gives employees more support when they need it.

Cons: An annual appraisal sets out clear objectives for employees to aim for. When these are attained there is a sense of achievement. That may disappear.

The feedback depends on the manager who may not remember to give it if the time and place are not clearly set out.

Exercise 3

Ask students to read the quote. Students can discuss this question in pairs before comparing answers with the rest of the class.

Possible answers

The company could ask for some input from you before the assessment: how the year has gone; what you feel was successful; what could have been done better.

The assessment should not be about comparing employees' performances.

The person holding the performance-development process should be thinking about the employees' strengths and not just looking at it from the company's point of view.

Task

Exercise 1

Ask students to work with a partner. They look at the table and think of three job roles, either in their company or in any company. It may be a good idea to encourage them to think of three quite different roles, for example, in sales, in administration, in research and design, so that the contents of the table do not become repetitive. They can then think of the responsibilities of each role and make notes in the table. They can repeat the process for the results and behaviour expected.

Exercise 2

When students have completed the table in **1**, ask the pairs to think of three simple performance measures for each of the roles. Remind them to keep measures simple. You could ask students if they have heard of SMART targets – these can be used to provide a more comprehensive definition of goal-setting. Suggestions for the acronym are:

S – specific, significant, stretching

M – measurable, meaningful, motivational

A – agreed upon, attainable, achievable, acceptable, action-orientated

R – relevant to the employee and their objectives

T – time bound, a set date, deadline by when the measure will be assessed

If students have heard of these, they could use them as a basis for the evaluation criteria. If students haven't heard of them, you could ask them to find out about the acronyms online.

Exercise 3

Students work in small groups, preferably not in the pairs they worked in for **1** and **2**. They tell the group about the roles, responsibilities, results, behaviours and measures they discussed in **1** and **2**. They can then discuss how realistic the measures for improvement are, and decide whether performance reviews or an informal approach would work better in developing people in their roles.

At the end of the discussion, you could ask students to assess the information in their table and their evaluation criteria. How would they assess their performance of the task? Dictate or write these questions on the board:

Are the responsibilities for each role clear? Are they different for each role? Is there a possibility of unnecessary duplication?

Are the results expected achievable? Can they be achieved in the timeframes given?

Is the behaviour expected reasonable?

Are the performance measures clear and simple?

Are they attainable in the time frame?

Give feedback on the language as well as on the achievement of the task.

ONE-TO-ONE Your student can read the *Context* and article, and then you can do the *Discussion* questions together. Ask your student to complete the tables in **1** and **2**. When the student has done this, ask him/her to present his/her ideas. Listen to the presentation and ask some difficult questions to get him/her to explain how realistic the measures for improvement are, and which style of review would be the most successful in his/her company.

PRE-WORK LEARNERS Ask students to work in groups of three and imagine they work in a large company. Ask each member of the group to think of a role and complete the table for one of the roles. If they find this hard, they could go to a large company website and look up the information. Then ask them to think of a simple performance measure for the role they chose, as in **2**.

They then work in small groups and tell the group about the role they chose, its responsibilities, results, behaviours, and the measures in **2**. They can then discuss how realistic the measures for improvement are, and decide whether performance reviews or an informal approach would work better in developing people in their roles.

At the end of the discussion, you could ask students to assess the information in their table and their evaluation criteria using the questions in the feedback after **3**.

9 Resources

Unit content

By the end of this unit, students will be able to
- talk about Corporate Social Responsibility (CSR)
- discuss options using conditionals
- avoid misunderstandings.

Context

The topic of *Resources* is fairly complex, due to the fact that the term can be interpreted in several ways. Generally speaking, 'resources' refers to a supply of something that a country, organization or person can use. Your students will relate fairly easily to the concept of the 'natural resources' provided by the world around us (e.g. minerals), but they may be less familiar with the resources of an organization. The resources available to a company are generally divided into four categories: physical (e.g. buildings); financial (e.g. funds available); human (e.g. staff); and intangible (e.g. brands).

In today's business world, it is important for a company not only to manage its own resources effectively, but also to be seen to support the sustainability of natural resources. Bad press on environmental issues can really damage a company's reputation. Many companies demonstrate their attitude towards managing resources (both natural resources and company resources) through Corporate Social Responsibility (CSR) projects. These usually involve working towards minimizing harm to the environment and benefiting local communities.

The first part of the unit looks at different resource types and how they can be managed, and gives information on how an international company is working to improve its environmental image. *Business communication* gives students practice in discussing feasibility and evaluating options. They then focus on the use of conditionals to make suggestions, express regret and deal with misunderstandings. In the *Viewpoint* video lesson, students find out about executive education and training in business. They are given information about a business education centre, the Saïd Business School, which is part of the University of Oxford, and have the opportunity to present a pitch for the Centre for Entrepreneurship and its scholarship to a prospective audience.

Starting point

For question 1, draw a spider diagram on the board with two legs. Write *resources* in the middle, write *natural resources* on the left-hand leg, and *company resources* on the right-hand leg.

Ask students to work in pairs or small groups and brainstorm examples for each category. Then write their ideas on the board.

Students then work in pairs and discuss question 2. Before doing this, make sure that students understand *intangible* (something that exists, but is difficult to describe, understand, or measure).

Possible answers

1 Natural resources: oil, gold, silver, copper, wood, cotton, coal, gas, water, wind, clay
Company resources: employees, money, buildings, land, brands, equipment, loans and credit agreements

2 Natural resources: pressures on these are usually the result of over-exploitation. Managing how much (and how often) a resource is used helps to relieve pressures on it.
Company resources: may experience the following types of pressure:
Financial pressures: ability to raise funds; instability in financial markets or value of commodities
Managed by careful financial planning, having clear goals for investors to understand, having a good record of financial stability
Human pressures: ability to recruit new and suitably qualified staff; unethical behaviour; over-exploitation
Managed by having good HR systems, having good organizational and management structures, having good training programmes, having an ethical policy on employment, having an ethical policy on working practices
Physical pressures: size of production facilities; IT hardware and software capabilities; natural disasters
Managed by having good planning and logistics, making sure production is sited in the best possible place with good transport links, having economies of scale, having a dedicated IT department, keeping abreast of IT developments, having emergency plans for natural disasters that are likely in your area, for example, in Japan what to do in earthquakes, in the UK having flood defences
Intangible pressures: perceptions and attitudes/damaged reputation
Managed by placing great importance on good customer relations, by reacting to problems/issues quickly and transparently, apologizing and rectifying company errors quickly and honestly

Working with words

Exercise 1

Students read the article and check their ideas from *Starting point*.

Before they read, you might want to check that students understand the following:

flagship = the most important product, service, building, etc. that an organization owns or produces

inauguration = the introduction of a new development or an important change

underwritten = accepted financial responsibility for an activity so that you will pay for special costs or for losses it may make

offset = to use one cost, payment or situation in order to cancel or reduce the effect of another

Exercise 2

Students work with a partner and discuss the questions.

Possible answers
1 Benefits to Michelin: It has a guarantee that a percentage of the rubber has to be sold to Michelin and this could be beneficial as demand for rubber is increasing and prices are rising. Indirectly, Michelin's image will be enhanced as the project will benefit the local community and so may attract new customers.
   Benefits to the local community: Secure jobs, allowing people to learn more about the business, improved living conditions, gaining experience of managing a profitable project; better economic conditions could lead to better social benefits such as improved schooling and healthcare.
2 Potential disadvantages to Michelin: Production of rubber is still low so supply is limited. The project also provides rubber for its competitors.
   Potential disadvantages to local community: If not managed correctly, Michelin could be seen as exploiting the local community, which could lose out economically and socially.

Exercise 3

Students replace the words in italics in questions 1–8 with a phrase in bold in the text in **1**. Then with a partner they can answer the questions.

Answers
1 natural resources	5 corporate accountability
2 endangered species	6 sustainable development
3 knowledge base	7 track record
4 critical success factor	8 CSR programme

DICTIONARY SKILLS

Ask students to work in pairs. Each pair should use a monolingual dictionary.

Ask students to find two words in the dictionary that collocate with *development, resource* or *factor*. Ask them to make sure they understand the collocation and then to use the pronunciation information in the dictionary to help them practise saying the words. They can then put the collocations in a sentence. When they are ready, ask students to say their sentences for the rest of the class and give feedback on their pronunciation.

Exercise 4

▶ **9.1** Students listen to three people talking about CSR and answer the questions. They can check their answers with a partner.

Answers
1 She's a shareholder, and wants to make her own decisions about donations and investments. She wants good long-term investments, and believes some CSR projects are not profitable in the long term.
2 CSR projects can really enhance the reputation and therefore the brand of a company.
3 Before signing an agreement, they ask for a cost-benefit analysis to ensure long-term project viability. They also make sure they can visit the site, and that they'll get reports and data relating to the project on a regular basis.

Exercise 5

Students work with a partner to complete sentences 1–9 with phrases from the list.

Answers
1 cost-benefit analysis	6 assets
2 drain on resources	7 short-term profit
3 long-term viability	8 market value
4 return on investment	9 bottom line
5 quantifiable data	

EXTENSION Ask students to choose a large company they know (and/or their own company). Ask them to find out about its CSR programme for homework. They can then report back on this in the next lesson.

Further practice
If students need more practice, go to *Practice file 9* on page 118 of the *Student's Book*.

Exercise 6

Students work in pairs. Allow time for them to read about the four projects. They should then discuss each project and think of the possible pros and cons for the current employees, the customers and the shareholders. Encourage students to use the language from **3** and **5**.

When they are ready, each pair can summarize their discussion for the rest of the class. Ask students to decide which group of people benefits most from each project and why.

Monitor their use of language. After the activity, give positive feedback on the correct use of vocabulary from **3** and **5**.

Possible answers

Project 1

Pros: current employees: improved knowledge base means each staff member will have improved their skills and therefore their career prospects

shareholders: maximizes use of human resources, and ultimately should result in an improvement to the bottom line and a good return on investment

customers: improved knowledge base of staff will mean a better service is provided

Cons: current employees: staff less comfortable with IT might struggle

shareholders: initial outlay of funds will affect the short-term profits

customers: staff might not be available when you need them – they'll be in training

Project 2

Pros: current employees: offers potential for promotion; reduces likelihood of having to do menial tasks

shareholders: putting local resources to good use could mean an improvement to the company's bottom line

customers: optimizing local resources – customers will see this as a benefit to the community (providing training and employment), so may be more likely to support the company

Cons: current employees: may feel their jobs are in jeopardy

shareholders: neither short-term profit nor return on investment is clear or guaranteed; could be seen as wasting or mismanaging resources: why not use current staff?

customers: may find themselves doing business with people with inadequate language skills

Project 3

Pros: current employees: benefits to health and fitness if staff walk or cycle to work

shareholders: increased market credibility due to clear concern for the environment

customers: will appreciate concern for the environment, and so may be more likely to support the company

Cons: current employees: some may live far from work and may not have access to public transport; will cause disruption during building works

shareholders: solar panels are very expensive – needs a cost-benefit analysis to decide if this has long-term viability

customers: product/service prices may increase due to costs of project

Project 4

Pros: current employees: current customer service staff may be offered alternative positions within the company

shareholders: increased market credibility due to clear concern for fair pay in developing countries

customers: may be more inclined to support the company

Cons: current employees: some will lose their jobs

shareholders: a cost-benefit analysis will be necessary to ensure long-term viability

customers: may have to deal with non-native speakers; accents and language issues may be problematic and this may be considered a mismanagement of resources

Exercise 7

Students discuss the projects in **6** in small groups. If they all work for different companies, they can share information about the projects and make suggestions together.

PRE-WORK LEARNERS Write the following questions on the board. Ask students to work in groups of three or four and discuss the questions.

- *Do you know any companies that have started similar projects to those in **6**? If so, tell your group what you know about it.*
- *Which of the projects would encourage you to work for a company that implemented them? Why?*

Photocopiable worksheet

Download and photocopy *Unit 9 Working with words worksheet* from the teacher resources in the *Online practice*.

Business communication

Exercise 1

Ask students to read the *Context* about Floralope and then discuss the question as a class.

Possible answers

Issues to consider include the availability of funds (financial resources); IT equipment and office/factory space (physical resources); trained staff and/or the possibility of recruiting them (human resources).

Exercise 2

▶ **9.2–9.5** Students listen to the extracts from the meeting. They should check their ideas in **1** and answer the questions. Before they listen, you might want to check that students understand the following:

reputable = that people consider to be honest and to provide a good service

outlay = the money that you have to spend in order to start a new project

Answers

1 The speakers discuss human, financial and physical resources.
2 Staff will need training, but overall human resources are not problematic. Although the buildings are quite run-down, they agree it can support the new system.
3 Margit takes a positive lead – she directs the conversation through the various points on the agenda, using words such as *so*, *now*, *OK*, etc., and summarizes the conversation on a regular basis.
4 Judit seems quite negative throughout. She is very direct, and always focuses on the problems or difficult issues.

Exercise 3

▶ **9.2–9.5** Students listen again and complete expressions a–l.

Answers
- **a** a long-term perspective
- **b** a clear strategy
- **c** a number of options
- **d** the bigger picture
- **e** our options are quite clear
- **f** How would it work if
- **g** a really strong position
- **h** don't have much choice / we can either / or we
- **i** the long-term viability
- **j** the general consensus is
- **k** points to consider
- **l** we're decided

Exercise 4

Students match the underlined expressions to questions a–c.

Answers
- **a** 1, 3, 6
- **b** 2, 4, 5
- **c** 2, 3, 6

> **Further practice**
> If students need more practice, go to *Practice file 9* on page 118 of the *Student's Book*.

Exercise 5

Students work in groups of four. Each pair within the group should turn to their information, Students A and B on page 73 of the *Student's Book* and Students C and D on page 139, and discuss the advantages of their proposals. When they are ready, they should join with the other pair and have the meeting. Refer them to the *Key expressions*. They should use the agenda to guide their discussion and should aim to reach a decision.

Monitor how they are using the *Key expressions*. For feedback, write three examples of how the expressions were used well, and three that were used incorrectly on the board. Ask students to decide which are incorrect, and how to improve them.

ONE-TO-ONE Ask the student to look at the information for Students A and B and you look at the information for Students C and D on page 139. Discuss the advantages of the new suggestions. Remind the student to use the *Key expressions*. Follow the agenda and try to reach a decision. When you have practised the meeting, ask the student to think about his/her company and about its strategies for IT, Marketing or investment that would enable expansion and explain them to you.

Exercise 6

Students work in pairs and discuss the projects. If possible, students should work with someone from the same company. If they are from different companies, they can focus on each company in turn.

PRE-WORK LEARNERS Students should discuss the projects in relation to a company they know or the college/university where they are studying.

Exercise 7

Each pair should now summarize their ideas for the rest of the class. You could ask students to prepare a PowerPoint presentation to give to the rest of the class answering the questions in **6**.

Encourage them to keep the information on each slide fairly minimal, using bullet points only. They can give their presentations in the next lesson.

Monitor how successful the meetings were. Make a note of any good use of the language from the *Key expressions* and give positive feedback at the end of the task.

> **Photocopiable worksheet**
> Download and photocopy *Unit 9 Business communication worksheet* from the teacher resources in the *Online practice*.

Language at work

Exercise 1

Students read the sentences and underline the verbs.

Answers
1. is, 'll be
2. check out, 'm, can find, will work
3. 's, investing, don't have
4. 'd invested, would have knocked down, had … built
5. made, could … train up
6. 'd recruited, would have had
7. had, could use, could … cope
8. hadn't invested, 'd be
9. work, can … improve

Exercise 2

Students work in pairs, and match the sentences in **1** to categories a–f.

Answers
a 1, 2, 9   **b** 5   **c** 3   **d** 7   **e** 4, 6   **f** 8

EXTENSION Write the sentences below on the board. Ask students to identify the forms in each sentence (answers are underlined). Then ask them to identify the conditional type (answers are in brackets).

1 If *interest rates go up, people save* more.
Form = If + subject + present simple + subject + present simple. (zero conditional)

2 If *I take* the job in marketing, I *will work* with Paul.
Form = If + subject + present simple + subject + will + infinitive. (first conditional)

3 If *we did* some research, *we could find out* what our customers want.
Form = If + subject + past simple + subject + could / would / might + infinitive. (second conditional)

4 If *I had listened* to my parents, *I would have studied* law.
Form = If + subject + past perfect + subject + could / would / might + have + past participle. (third conditional)

5 If *I hadn't spent* so much money on clothes, I *wouldn't be* in debt now.
Form = If + subject + past perfect + subject + could / would / might + infinitive. (mixed)

Exercise 3

Students match the sentences in **1** to the categories in **2**. Then ask them to see if they can notice any patterns.

Answers

zero: 3	3rd: 4, 6
1st: 1, 2, 9	mixed: 8
2nd: 5, 7	

Students should notice the following:

- Zero conditionals are used to talk about facts.
- First conditionals are used to predict the results of a likely future event.
- Second conditionals are used to predict the results of a less likely future event, or to hypothesize/suggest.
- Third conditionals are used to talk about past regrets or relief about things which didn't actually happen.
- Mixed conditionals are used to express the present effects of a past decision/action.

Grammar reference

If students need more information, go to *Grammar reference* on page 131 of the *Student's Book*.

Exercise 4

Students work in pairs and take turns to discuss the situations using conditional forms to talk about the past, present and future consequences.

Possible answers

1 If we start cutting costs now, we might not go bankrupt / we may be saved from bankruptcy.
2 If we raise interest rates, consumer spending may drop.
3 If we hadn't hired Ian, those people probably wouldn't have left.
4 If I hadn't gone into this profession, I wouldn't be bored now.
5 If I was one of the ones relocated to Berlin, I'd be able to meet up with my friends more often. (less likely) / If I'm located to Berlin, I'll be able to … (more likely)
6 If I can negotiate a good salary increase, we'll be able to go to the Caribbean!

Further practice

If students need more practice, go to *Practice file 9* on page 119 of the *Student's Book*.

Exercise 5

Students work in pairs and turn to page 138 of the *Student's Book*. Allow time for them to read the information. They should then discuss what happened, using conditionals where appropriate.

Possible answers

1 If we hadn't invested in new equipment, we wouldn't have been able to increase the membership fee.
  If we had developed a competitive special offer in January, we wouldn't have lost potential customers to the competition.
2 If we had addressed the HR crisis, we would have more trainers now, and our current trainers wouldn't be overworked. We wouldn't have so many customers on our waiting list.
  If we hadn't developed the local school partnership, we wouldn't have overweight teenagers on our fitness programme now.
3 (These answers can be in first or second conditional depending on their likelihood.)
  If we can develop new membership packages, we'll increase member numbers.
  If we start more initiatives with teenagers, we'll improve the gym's reputation and get new young members.
  If we employ more trainers, we'll make more profit from tailor-made personal programmes.
  If we renovated the pool, we'd have a better reputation and we'd be able to put our prices up.

Exercise 6

Students make notes about the past year and next year in their company, department or team. They then discuss their notes in pairs, using appropriate conditional forms. Encourage them to use the full range of conditional sentences to express their thoughts and ideas.

As you monitor the students, acknowledge good use of the conditional sentences. Make a note of any problems and deal with them at the end of the activity.

Possible answers

1 If we hadn't won that contract, we wouldn't have had to work every evening and weekend.
2 If John hadn't left, he would be the first person I'd ask to help me!
3 If we give our staff more language training, they'll be able to deal more effectively with our international customers. If we were allowed to work from home, we would save time and petrol expenses, but we would still be able to communicate easily on the phone and by email.

PRE-WORK LEARNERS Ask students to think about their past year of studies and their plans for next year.

EXTRA ACTIVITY

Write the four prompts below on cards. Prepare a set for every two students in your class. Ask students to work in pairs and take turns to interview each other using the prompts on the cards to form conditionals. Encourage students to ask further questions to find out more.

- *chance to study abroad / take it?*
- *study something different / job now?*
- *any role in the company of your dreams / what? why?*
- *study again / what? why?*

Example: *If you were given the chance to study abroad, would you take it?*

When they have finished, ask students to report back on what they found out.

Photocopiable worksheet

Download and photocopy *Unit 9 Language at work worksheet* from the teacher resources in the *Online practice*.

Practically speaking

Exercise 1

▶ **9.6** Students listen to five conversations and answer the questions.

Remind students that intonation and language (usually longer phrases) help to identify politeness.

> **Possible answers**
> 1 polite = 1, 2, 4
> 2 less polite = 3, 5

Exercise 2

▶ **9.6** Students listen again and mark the phrases a–l, according to the conversations (1–5) they are heard in.

> **Answers**
> **a** 3 **b** 3 **c** 2 **d** 1 **e** 5 **f** 3 **g** 4 **h** 4 **i** 5 **j** 2
> **k** 5 **l** 5

Exercise 3

Students work in pairs and answer the questions.

> **Answers**
> 1 Direct: a, b, e, f, i, k
>   Less direct: c, d, g, h, j, l
> 2 Sorry; I was thinking … / What I actually wanted to say … / What I meant was … / It may seem … / That's not exactly …
> 3 You might want to be less direct when speaking to someone senior to you; when you know you've made a mistake; when you want to clarify something.
>   You might want to be more direct when the mistake/misunderstanding has occurred more than once before; when the phone line is bad and you need to make yourself understood; when speaking to someone from a culture where they are more direct.

Exercise 4

Students change the phrases to make them less direct using words from the list.

> **Possible answers**
> 1 That's not exactly what I meant – I actually said …
> 2 I didn't quite mean that, actually.
> 3 Actually, I'm not sure exactly what you mean.
> 4 (Sorry, but) I'm not really sure what you're talking about.
> 5 Actually, that's not exactly right.

> **EXTRA ACTIVITY**
> Write the sentence below on the board. Then tell students that you are going to say the sentence in three ways and they should decide which is the most polite.
> *That's not exactly what I meant, I actually said …*
> Say the sentence in the following three ways:
> 1 Say *exactly* and *actually* with very flat intonation.
> 2 Stress *exactly* and *actually* naturally to sound quite polite.
> 3 Exaggerate the stress on *exactly* and *actually*, with wide intonation, to sound very polite.

Useful phrases

Refer students to the *Useful phrases* section on page 135 of the *Student's Book* for extension and revision.

Exercise 5

Students work in pairs. Student A and Student B take turns to deal with the misunderstanding using the phrases in **2**. Remind students to think about their intonation. Do they sound polite?

While monitoring students, pay particular attention to their intonation. Give feedback after the activity.

Exercise 6

Students work in pairs, making complaints or suggestions and dealing with any misunderstanding in the situations given.

> **CULTURE QUESTION**
> Students can discuss the questions as a class. You could also explore how different cultures value directness or indirectness. To generate discussion, write the countries listed below on the board. Ask students to decide which ones tend to value directness (D) and which tend to value indirectness (I). Can they add any other countries to the list?
> (Some suggested answers are in brackets, but these are only tendencies so handle this with sensitivity.)
> - *Portugal* (I)
> - *Sweden* (D)
> - *Holland* (D)
> - *Indonesia* (I)
> - *Britain* (I)
>
> You could ask students to find out about a country of their choice online.

> **KEY WORD**
> Students match the uses of *look* in sentences 1–5 to the definitions a–e.
> > **Answers**
> > **1** d **2** a **3** c **4** e **5** b

Progress test

Download and photocopy *Unit 9 Progress test* and *Speaking test* from the teacher resources in the *Online practice*.

Viewpoint 3

Exercise 1

Before students watch the video, ask them to match the words and phrases 1–9 from the videos to their definitions a–i.

Answers
1 d 2 b 3 f 4 h 5 c 6 e 7 a 8 g 9 i

Exercise 2

Students complete the questions with words and phrases from **1** and check their answers with a partner.

Answers
1 on the hoof
2 up and running
3 time out
4 spark off
5 social impact / transformational

Exercise 3

Students take turns to ask and answer the questions in **2**.

Exercise 4

▶ 01 Students watch Kathy Harvey answering three different questions and put them in order.

Answers
A 3 B 2 C 1

Exercise 5

▶ 01 Students watch the video again and answer the questions. They can then discuss their answers with a partner.

Answers
1 They're trying to transform themselves in a complex way, to learn more, to build on their skills and refresh their thinking.
2 They need time out to refresh their thinking so they can create new frameworks to view old problems, think about things differently and take action.
3 multifaceted learning – a mixture of online, conversations, peer-learning through discussion and seminars, reflection and lectures
4 She says that executives learn from each other. She says peer-learning is vital because executives have a lot to offer and so have a lot to learn from each other.
5 a social venture in Africa
6 the lives of the group of students and of many of their clients

Exercise 6

Students discuss the questions in groups.

PRE-WORK LEARNERS Ask students to think about their own learning situation, both academic and any other situations, for example, sports, musical, dramatic, first aid training.

Exercise 7

▶ 02 Students watch four short interviews with people who work at the Skoll Centre and make notes in the table. They then compare their notes with a partner.

Answers
1 It is a leading centre for the advancement of social innovation, based in the Saïd Business School, University of Oxford.
2 It provides students with a launch in their social impact careers by teaching them ways in which they can get involved and helps them with their social ventures and their businesses.
3 'Leading for Impact'
4 It funds people who have been working in the social impact sector, who have success as an entrepreneur, or someone who has pursued a portfolio career that has focused on a certain social or environmental issue.

Exercise 8

▶ 03 Students watch four short interviews with people who study at the Skoll Centre and make notes in the table. They then compare their notes with a partner. Students could do some research online if they wish to find out more about the projects mentioned.

Answers
1 Because it offers a great deal of resources for networking and self-development. It also gives students the opportunity to do an entrepreneurship project and has invaluable resources.
2 It has amazing facilities for students to learn about the industry.
3 energy and a language programme
4 A non-profit organization called 'Better Livelihoods Uganda', which tries to use market approaches to address social problems.

Exercise 9

Each student prepares a two-minute pitch for the centre using the information in the videos in **7** and **8**. Remind them that they are going to promote the centre and its scholarship to an audience of potential students.

Exercise 10

Students work in pairs. They take turns to give their pitches. As they listen to their partner, they should make notes for the questions and give feedback to the speaker after both have given their pitches.

Further ideas and video scripts

You can find a list of suggested ideas for how to use video in the class in the teacher resources in the *Online practice*. The video scripts are available to download from the Teaching Resources on the Oxford Teachers' Club. www.oup.com/elt/teacher/businessresult

10 Leadership

Unit content

By the end of this unit, students will be able to

- discuss types of leadership
- give a briefing using the passive
- say how they feel about something.

Context

Leadership is a topic that everyone can relate to. Even if someone hasn't had any leadership experience, they will have been led by good or bad managers at some point. It is important to note that there is a difference between the terms *leadership* and *management*. Whereas managers tend to have colleagues and work in teams, leaders are those who see the bigger picture, and have the vision and commitment to make radical changes. Leaders are usually creative and innovative, always looking for new solutions to problems, and it is often the managers who are called on to implement the leaders' ideas.

There are a variety of leadership styles, and your students may well have had different experiences depending on their nationality and the types of organization they have worked in. An autocratic style of leadership is one where the leader gives instructions to their subordinates. Conversely, a democratic leader will share the responsibility, involving others in the decision-making. A laissez-faire style involves minimal supervision, and allows employees to take the initiative and make decisions.

The first part of this unit allows discussion of different leadership qualities and examines which are typical in different national cultures. Students are then given the opportunity to practise a typical management task – giving an effective briefing to staff. They are also encouraged to use passive forms to help depersonalize the information. The *Talking point* is about how you can take the lead in a situation even when you are not the manager/official leader. Students have the opportunity to present an idea to the group and then convince them to implement their idea.

Starting point

Discuss the first question as a class. Write the names of the people mentioned on the board and encourage students to describe the leadership qualities that they think each person has. They can then discuss questions 2–3 in pairs.

Possible answers

1 Students' own answers
2 Answers will vary. Some may argue that skills can be learnt through experience, age and management training courses. Others may believe that the skills are dependent on personalities and therefore cannot be learnt.
3 A *leader* is a person who leads a group of people, especially the head of a country, an organization, etc. They are more concerned with 'the bigger picture' rather than day-to-day events.
A *manager* is a person who is in charge of running a company department, a business, a shop/store or a similar organization. They usually work with teams and therefore need to be people-focused.

Working with words

Exercise 1

Students work in pairs. They read the first paragraph of an article by a leadership coach and discuss the questions.

Exercise 2

Students read the rest of the article and compare the writer's suggestions with their ideas in **1**.

Answers

The writer gives various suggestions for making sure this style doesn't happen: Firstly, he suggests that managers stop communicating by smartphone and meet and talk to staff. This gives the manager a more people-focused approach. It also allows the manager to connect with the energy and enthusiasm of the staff who are generally happy to be consulted. They will come up with new ideas, which the manager actually listens to and engages with. The manager needs to demonstrate an open-minded approach and create a culture of continuous improvement. When the manager does this, he/she shows integrity. The manager can show decisiveness and the staff will feel included in the decision. This does not need to take more time, simply cut long unproductive formal meetings and have shorter productive discussions.

Exercise 3

Students read the article again and match the adjectives and nouns in bold from the texts to the quotes.

Answers

1	humble	7	conviction
2	decisive	8	adaptable
3	empathy	9	integrity
4	self-aware	10	collaborative
5	commitment	11	hands-off
6	passionate	12	people-focused

Write the words from **3** on the board as indicated below. Ask students to indicate the stress on each word (see underlined sections below for the answers). Then elicit the noun form of each adjective, the verb form of *empathy*, *conviction* and *collaborative*, and the adjective from *commitment* (answers are in brackets). Ask students to check their ideas in a dictionary and to find out the word stress for the new words.

Answers
1 humble (humility)
2 decisive (decision)
3 empathy (empathize)
4 self-aware (self-awareness)
5 commitment (committed)
6 passionate (passion)
7 conviction (convince)
8 adaptable (adaptability, adaptation)
9 integrity
10 collaborative (collaboration, collaborate)
11 hands-off
12 people-focused

EXTENSION Write the following pairs of adjectives on the board. Ask students to match each pair of adjectives to an adjective in **3** with the opposite meaning (answers are in brackets).

1 *interfering, controlling* (*hands-off*)
2 *inflexible, rigid* (*adaptable*)
3 *hesitant, indecisive* (*decisive*)
4 *directive, top-down* (*collaborative*)
5 *apathetic, unenthusiastic* (*passionate*)
6 *autocratic, task-orientated* (*people-focused*)

Exercise 4

Students work in pairs and read the information on page 142 of the *Student's Book*. They then prepare a short verbal report describing the leadership styles. You might like to write the following sentence starters on the board to help them:

Positive	Negative
He/She's quite/very … *He/She has …* *He/She shows a lot of …*	*He/She's not very …* *He/She lacks/has a lack of …* *He/She's not able to show …*

Answers
Team leader A: He/she's good at achieving results, and shows a lot of commitment. He/she is decisive, and is very good at delegating. However, he/she's not very good at consulting on decisions, and doesn't have much empathy. He/she also lacks self-awareness and is not able to demonstrate flexibility.
Team leader B: He/she is very results-orientated and shows commitment. He/she can be trusted, and has a participative style. He/she is able to communicate well, and is very people-orientated. However, he/she lacks the ability to be decisive. Team leader B seems to show much better team-leading skills.

Dictate the following descriptions of teams for students to write down. Encourage students to ask for spellings if required. Ask students to work in small groups and decide what kind of team leader would be best for each team and why.

- *Team 1: a team with lax discipline, high absenteeism, and a generally sloppy way of working – this has led to low levels of productivity.*
- *Team 2: a team where most participants work independently, only consulting each other when absolutely necessary. They stick closely to their remit and get the job done on time, but the atmosphere at work is often fairly cold.*
- *Team 3: a team where participants try to get their tasks done as quickly as possible, though not necessarily doing them well. Cliques are forming within the team and there seems to be an atmosphere of back-stabbing and colluding, resulting in some team members withdrawing and not contributing as much as they could.*

Exercise 5

Students work in pairs and discuss the questions.

PRE-WORK LEARNERS Encourage students with minimal or no work experience to talk about their experience of leaders and leadership styles in teams outside work/study places, e.g. teams in sports, music, clubs, etc.

Exercise 6

▶ **10.1–10.2** Students listen to two people talking about becoming a team leader and answer the questions.
Before students listen, you might want to check that they understand the following:
fuselage = the main part of an aircraft in which passengers and goods are carried
micromanage = to control in a detailed way (negative)

Answers
1 Both were put in charge of a team they didn't know well, and needed to develop trust.
In Lydia's team, the team members didn't work very closely together, and had relied heavily on their previous team leader. Lydia decided she needed to build up trust over time and reduce competition among them to develop cohesion.
Bruce had little control over his team because they mostly reported to other people. He realized he had to establish his credibility and find out what was important for each individual, show an interest in them and support them, in order to ensure that they were motivated.
2 Students' own answers

Exercise 7

▶ **10.1–10.2** Students match 1–12 to a–l to make phrases. Ask students to compare their answers in pairs. Then play the listening again to check which combinations were used. Elicit additional possible combinations from students.

Answers
1 f 2 j 3 h 4 a 5 b 6 l 7 c 8 k 9 d 10 g
11 e 12 i

Other possible combinations:
3 g, k, l 4 h, k, l 5/6 g, h, k, l 7 b 8 g, h, k 12 a, b, h, k

Further practice

If students need more practice, go to *Practice file 10* on page 120 of the *Student's Book*.

Exercise 8

Students work with a partner and discuss the advice they would give in the two situations. Encourage them to use vocabulary from **3** and **7**. You could then ask each pair to present advice for one of the situations for the rest of the class.

Exercise 9

Students work in small groups and discuss their own leadership styles.

Monitor and make a note of language used. Provide positive feedback on correct use of the vocabulary from this section.

> **CULTURE QUESTION**
> Discuss the questions as a class. You might like to also discuss the second question in relation to the cultures within companies.

Photocopiable worksheet

Download and photocopy *Unit 10 Working with words worksheet* from the teacher resources in the *Online practice*.

Business communication

Exercise 1

▶ **10.3** Ask students to read about Nordica in the *Context* and the meeting agenda. Elicit what the problem is (the technology of the e-banking system is not fully integrated) and what the proposed solution is (to implement a faster, new single system). Students then listen to Jim Brolin's briefing in part 1 of the meeting and answer the questions.

> **Possible answers**
> 1 It will bring all the applications together, resulting in a more personalized service for clients. It will also allow the business to grow more quickly in core markets.
> 2 a
> 3 a, c, d, f

Exercise 2

▶ **10.3** Students listen again and note down the expressions. Ask students to compare their answers with a partner. They can then work together to add any similar expressions.

> **Answers**
> 1 … a decision was taken at last week's strategy meeting
> … it has been agreed that we are going to combine …
> It is proposed that we hold a series of seminars …
> 2 What this will allow us to do is offer our clients … something we couldn't do before.
> Another great thing about this development is that …
> There may be some short-term inconvenience during the implementation and switchover phase, but it will be well worth the investment.
> 3 … you and your teams are crucial to the success of this strategy
> Each one of you has a key role to play in making the new system work.
> I'd like to see all of you being proactive and taking a lead in this.
> I would encourage all of you to do this.

Exercise 3

Students work with a partner and choose one of the topics. Allow time for them to discuss their topic and make notes to help them with their introduction to a briefing. Encourage them to use expressions from **2** in their briefing. When they are ready, ask pairs to present their introductions to the class.

After each presentation, ask the class the following questions, or write them on the board:

*   *Did you feel involved?*
*   *How did you feel about their approach (resentment / anxiety / solidarity / something else)?*

Exercise 4

▶ **10.4** Students listen to part 2 of the meeting and answer the questions. You might want to check that students understand the following words in the questions and the listening:

dismissive = showing that you do not believe a person or thing to be important or worth considering
reassuring = making you feel less worried or uncertain about something
recoup = to get back an amount of money that you have spent or lost

> **Answers**
> 1 They are concerned about timing and workload; getting the support to organize training for their teams; whether customers will be affected badly during the process; whether they will be asked to contribute from budgets.
> 2 He is reassuring. He acknowledges their concerns appropriately and explains how they will be dealt with. Where the solutions are less good, he focuses on the positive side, and tries to encourage them to do the same.

Exercise 5

▶ **10.4** Before they listen again, ask students to read the incomplete sentences. Ask them to discuss in pairs how they think the sentences could be completed. Then play the listening and ask students to complete the sentences.

> **Answers**
> 1 I'm slightly concerned about
> 2 I wonder if you have any information
> 3 I understand your concerns
> 4 I think we need to look at
> 5 As I understand it
> 6 I'm not very happy about
> 7 Can you give us an assurance that
> 8 That's a valid point
> 9 I really don't see this as a problem
> 10 My understanding is
> 11 I also have some concerns about
> 12 What assurances can you give us
> 13 I have some reservations about
> 14 Are there any guarantees that
> 15 I understand where you're coming from
> 16 Apparently
> 17 let's give this a chance to work

Exercise 6

Students match the expressions 1–17 in **5** to categories a–d. Students could check their answers against the *Key expressions* box.

> **Answers**
> **a** 1, 6, 11, 13
> **b** 2, 7, 12, 14
> **c** 3, 4, 8, 9, 15, 17
> **d** 5, 10, 16

Further practice

If students need more practice, go to *Practice file 10* on page 120 of the *Student's Book*.

Exercise 7

Students work in pairs and read the situations. Before they begin their discussion, ask them to brainstorm any potential problems relating to each situation and any additional positive points. Then ask them to take on A and B roles, and discuss the situations. Encourage them to use the language in the *Key expressions*.

Exercise 8

Each student should think of a possible change in their company. They then take turns to explain the change, whilst the other student takes notes and lists any concerns.

Monitor and make a note of any errors and any good use of the expressions from **5**. Give positive feedback to students who used expressions from **5** appropriately and correct any mistakes if necessary. Then ask students if their partner responded appropriately to their concerns and if not, how they could improve.

PRE-WORK LEARNERS As a class, brainstorm changes that could be made at the students' college/university. Use the following ideas if necessary:

- Increase/introduce tuition fees so that college/university facilities can be improved.
- Force students who miss more than four classes in one subject to leave the college/university.
- Abolish coursework – exams will form 100% of assessment.
- Introduce a strict fining system on overdue library books.

Photocopiable worksheet

Download and photocopy *Unit 10 Business communication worksheet* from the teacher resources in the *Online practice*.

Language at work

Exercise 1

Students look at sentences 1–8 and underline the passive forms.

> **Answers**
> **1** was taken
> **2** has been agreed
> **3** 've been given
> **4** will be coordinated, 'll be briefed
> **5** is proposed
> **6** 's been suggested, will be recouped
> **7** 've been told, need to be shared around
> **8** has already been made

Exercise 2

Students work in pairs. They look at the passive forms in sentences 1–8 in **1** and discuss the questions.

> **Answers**
> **1** was taken = past simple passive
>   has been agreed = present perfect passive
>   've been given = present perfect passive
>   will be coordinated, 'll be briefed = future passive
>   is proposed = present simple passive
>   's been suggested, will be recouped = present perfect passive, future passive
>   've been told, need to be shared around = present perfect passive, present simple passive (infinitive)
>   has already been made = present perfect passive
> **2** Answers will vary, although the following are likely:
>   a all, but especially 4 and 5
>   b 3
>   c 4
>   d 1, 2, 5, 6, 7, 8

Exercise 3

Students look at sentences a–b and answer the questions.

> **Answers**
> **1** b *(me)*
> **2** *me* in the active sentence becomes *I* in the passive – it becomes the subject of the passive sentence
> **3** no, because *suggest* does not take an indirect object, so *I* cannot be the subject here

Grammar reference

If students need more information, go to *Grammar Reference* on page 132 of the *Student's Book*.

Exercise 4

Students work with a partner. They take turns to report the information in the sentences in the passive using the correct form of the verbs in italics.

> **Possible answers**
> **1** I/we have been informed that …
> **2** It has been agreed that we should cut back on …
> **3** It has been proposed that the department is / will be restructured …
> **4** We have been instructed by Head Office to reduce our spending by 5%.
> **5** It has been decided that bonuses will be paid …
> **6** We've been persuaded to take part in a new system trial.

EXTENSION Ask students to choose one of the ideas in **4** and write an email to their staff about it.

Further practice

If students need more practice, go to *Practice file 10* on page 121 of the *Student's Book*.

Exercise 5

Students work with a partner and turn to the information on page 140 of the *Student's Book*. Allow time for them to read the memo. Ask them to underline the sections of the memo that would need to be depersonalized in a briefing meeting. Students should then think about how they would rephrase those sections in a briefing meeting. The following sections are most likely to need rephrasing:

- *We have approved …*
- *All members of staff at team leader grade and below will have to spend a minimum …*
- *We want all individuals to set up and schedule … / agree with their line manager …*
- *We will not allow extra time for work you don't complete.*
- *We expect that staff will cover for absent colleagues.*

Then ask pairs to give a short briefing to the rest of the class, rephrasing information where necessary.

Before students give their briefings to the class, divide them into two groups. Group A should listen and comment on how willing they think staff would be to participate in the job-shadowing initiative, based on the way the information is presented. Group B should listen and note down any correct and incorrect use of reporting verbs (*tell, inform, agree, decide,* etc.). After each briefing, elicit comments from the two groups.

EXTENSION Ask students to work with a partner and use the memo to help them write a briefing for staff in email format, rephrasing where necessary. Students then swap emails with another pair and write an email in reply, expressing their concerns. Pairs then swap emails again and write a response, dealing with the concerns.

Photocopiable worksheet
Download and photocopy *Unit 10 Language at work worksheet* from the teacher resources in the *Online practice*.

Practically speaking

Exercise 1
Students work with a partner and answer the questions.

Exercise 2
▶ 10.5 Students listen to three conversations and answer the questions.

> **Answers**
> Conversation 1: They are discussing a new assessment system. They are probably chatting over coffee after a meeting.
> Conversation 2: They are talking about one of the speakers' experiences in Kenya, and why they liked it. It could be part of an appraisal meeting between a manager and an employee, or it may be colleagues talking.
> Conversation 3: They are talking about dealing with attitudes and using a team-building weekend as an example. They could be at a meeting bringing together people from different departments of a big company.

Exercise 3
▶ 10.5 Before they listen again, students read the extracts. Ask them to try to complete the sentences. They can then listen again and check their ideas.

> **Answers**
> 1 to be honest with you   6 Honestly
> 2 personally speaking   7 Personally
> 3 I have to say   8 I look at it like this
> 4 to tell you the truth   9 my attitude is
> 5 To be perfectly honest

Useful phrases
Refer students to the *Useful phrases* section on page 136 of the *Student's Book* for extension and revision.

Exercise 4
Students work with a partner and answer the questions. They can then turn to audio script 10.5 on pages 156–157 to check their answers.

> **Answers**
> 1 In each case, the speaker's opinion follows. The phrases are used to let the listener know that you are expressing a personal opinion, or revealing your true thoughts. Sometimes they soften the tone, or indicate that a negative response will follow.
> 2 Speaker A uses the following phrases:
> *What did you think of …?*
> *Such as?*
> *You're not in favour of …?*
> *What did you like about it?*
> *It must have been challenging at times?*
> *How does it feel to be back at the centre of things?*
> *I heard some people thought it was a waste of time.*
> *What do you mean?*
> *So …?*

Exercise 5
Students work with a partner. Ask them to decide who is A, and who is B for each situation. Allow time for them to read the situations and form an opinion about the details. When they are ready, they should take turns to ask for and give their personal views. When students have finished, write the following questions on the board:

- *Did you have a chance to express your opinion?*
- *Were you prompted appropriately?*
- *How easy was it to ask questions to find out your partner's opinion?*
- *Did you use many of the phrases from exercise 3?*

Elicit answers to the questions from the whole class and discuss any ways in which they could be improved.

> **KEY WORD**
> Students read the sentences using *even* and answer the questions.
>
> **Answers**
> a In sentence 1 *even* emphasizes that something hasn't happened. In sentence 3 *even* emphasizes a comparison.
> b In sentence 2 *even so* can be replaced by *nevertheless*. In sentence 4 *even if* can be replaced by *despite the fact that*.

Ask students to work in groups of three. Write some topics on individual cards, making sure they will be suitable for your group. For example:

- *the state of the economy in your country*
- *the last film you saw / book you read*
- *the royal family in the UK*
- *the future of your company / college / university*
- *your first boss / your first English teacher*
- *your best/worst assignment*
- *your dream job*

Give each group a set of cards, face down. Students then take turns to take a card and begin talking about the topic. The other students should listen, and ask questions to prompt the speaker to give their opinions. They can then also express their own opinions.

Progress test

Download and photocopy *Unit 10 Progress test* and *Speaking test* from the teacher resources in the *Online practice*.

Talking point

Discussion

Exercise 1

Students work individually and make a list of the leadership skills they have. You could ask them to make a note of an example of where and when they demonstrated these.

Exercise 2

Allow a few minutes for students to read the *Context* and article. Be ready to answer any questions students may have about vocabulary.

Students work individually and compare the points in the article with their answers in **1**, deciding which they agree with and which would have an effect on their boss. They can then discuss their ideas with a partner, explaining the reasons for their answers.

Exercise 3

Students discuss with a partner the methods of persuasion that do and don't work for them.

Task

Exercise 1

Students work individually. They think of a change they would like to make at work. Ask them to think carefully about why they want to make the change and what the results of the change could be. Refer them back to the article so they remember the points it made about leadership and working with bosses and managers.

PRE-WORK LEARNERS Ask students to work individually and think of a change they think would benefit the college they study at. They should think carefully about why they want to make the change, who the change would benefit, and what the results of the change could be. Refer them back to the article but you may need to revise some of the headings, for example:

1 *Remember to frame your suggestion so that it doesn't simply benefit your class/group, but the whole college and the people who run the college.*

2 *Pay extra attention to the department's and the head of the department's problems.*

3–4 as in the article

5 *Look for ideas online. Read through other college brochures and see how things are done differently.*

6–9 as in the article

10 *If your head of department agrees to give it a try, do everything you can to make it work.*

Still working individually, students look at their list and transform the statements they made in **1** to appeal to the Department Heads in the college. Refer students to the *Key expressions* in *Business communication* on page 81 to help them with the preparation. Students can then move on to **3**.

Exercise 2

Still working individually, students look at their list and transform the statements they made in **1** to appeal to the board of directors. Refer students to the *Key expressions* in *Business communication* to help them with the preparation.

Exercise 3

Students now work in groups of four. They then each have a turn to outline their change and its potential benefits and persuade the group to implement their idea using the language from the unit. You could ask the other students to make brief notes while they listen, and ask questions to clarify the change and its possible results. They then decide on which ideas to implement. You could ask each group to present one of its ideas to the class.

Focus on the language that students use during the presentations. Give feedback on their use of passive forms and on the phrases they use to express and respond to concerns. Put any incorrect sentences on the board and ask the class to correct the mistakes.

ONE-TO-ONE The student can read the *Context* and the article, and then you can do the *Discussion* questions together. In the *Task* the student decides on one or two changes and their possible results and he/she tries to persuade you to implement one of them.

Ask students to explain their idea in an email addressed to 'All staff'. Students can then exchange emails and respond to each other, raising any concerns. The first student can then write a follow-up email to clarify potential benefits. You can then collect all the emails and provide feedback in the following lesson. Focus on common errors. You could also prepare a worksheet with a list of sentences from their emails. Students can then work in pairs to correct the mistakes.

Unit content

By the end of this unit, students will be able to

- discuss values
- reach an agreement using formal and emphatic language
- talk about difficult issues.

Context

A company's *Values* provide guidelines that can inform company decisions and activities. There is a growing trend in the business world not only to make the values of a company explicit to all staff, but also to use these values as a PR device. By publicizing their values, companies underline their corporate aims and help to build up trust amongst their customers.

Publicly-stated values are used to inform procedures and behaviour at all levels of the company. Indeed, many staff are now given training relating specifically to these values. Appraisal systems can also include adherence to company values as part of the performance objectives. Basing these measures on publicized values could be seen to strengthen the foundations of a company.

In the first part of this unit, students look at the language used to describe company values. They also have the opportunity to discuss what factors might affect public perception of these values. Students then move on to focus on the language used in negotiations and how to use participle clauses and inversion to emphasize a message and be more formal. The *Talking point* examines the idea of 'whistle-blowing' and scandal in business. Students read about a company president who went public with allegations of wrongdoing and was subsequently fired. Students have the opportunity to write a framework for a company's Code of Conduct.

Starting point

For question 1, ask students to work in pairs to come up with a definition of the term *values* (it's important this is in the plural). Students may mention the following meaning: *value* = how much something is worth in money. This is also correct, but this is not the focus of the unit. You might like to discuss the connection between this definition and the definition of *values* (i.e. both are related to the importance you place on something).

As a lead-in to questions 2 and 3, elicit what the values of a company could include. You could find out the values of a well-known company by researching on the Internet before the lesson. Then write the values on the board and ask students to explain what they think each value means in practice (e.g. offering excellent customer service, building good relationships with clients, employees and wider society). Students can then discuss questions 2, 3 and 4 with a partner.

Students can finish *Starting point* by discussing the values that are important to them with a partner.

Possible answers

1 values = beliefs about what is right and wrong and what is important in life
2 A company needs values so that it has a set of rules / rationale on which to base its decisions. It will also be able to use these values as a PR tool. Without clear values, companies are not able to be consistent; staff will be unable to perform effectively, and customers may be confused.
3 and 4 Students' own answers

Working with words

Exercise 1

Students work with a partner and discuss the questions on TATA. You could introduce a competitive element to the first question, giving points to each group for correct answers.

You could ask students to find information about the company online. Divide the class into two groups. Tell one group they could look at the TATA website and make notes on how the company describes itself. The other group finds articles and information online that is independent of the company and makes notes. The groups can then compare notes on TATA and decide on the values the company shows.

Answers

1 TATA is an Indian multinational conglomerate holding company, with interests in seven business sectors, including airlines, cars, steel and engineering services.
2 and 3 Students' own answers

Exercise 2

Students read the values statements from TATA and match the core values to the explanations 1–5. Ask them to compare their ideas with a partner.

Answers
1 Integrity
2 Responsibility
3 Excellence
4 Pioneering
5 Unity

Exercise 3

Students read the 'Our Employees' section from the *TATA Code of Conduct* and match the words in bold in the section to the definitions 1–8.

Answers
1 mutual cooperation
2 merit
3 respect
4 diversity
5 competence
6 dignity
7 equality
8 tolerance

Exercise 4

Students work with a partner. They read the sections from the *TATA Code of Conduct* again and discuss them in relation to their own company.

EXTENSION Students might not know what the values of their company are – ask them to research this for the next lesson.

PRE-WORK LEARNERS Ask students to look at two companies in their country and their company statements, and decide which company they would prefer to work for, based on the values statement. Encourage them to give reasons.

Exercise 5

▶ 11.1 Before they listen, ask students to tell you which big American companies they know of, for example, Coca-Cola, Starbucks, Uber, Nike, Microsoft, Boeing, Morgan Stanley, and what they know about the companies. Ask students what their attitudes are to American companies (positive/negative) and why. Students then listen and answer the questions.

Answers
1 Recent American foreign policy is thought to be controversial. There have been several corporate financial scandals. It has a poor environmental record. It has lost its moral authority.
2 Fewer people are buying American brands.
3 Other economic factors could be the reason and European brands are also suffering from lower sales.

Exercise 6

Students match the adverb + adjective combinations from the discussion in **5** to the statements 1–8 that are closest in meaning.

Answers
1 increasingly difficult
2 relatively stable
3 significantly different
4 unexpectedly rapid
5 potentially disastrous
6 appreciably more hostile
7 profoundly worrying
8 irretrievably damaging

PRONUNCIATION Ask students to mark the stress on the adverb + adjective combinations (answers underlined below). They can check the stress in a dictionary. When students have done that, ask them to work with a partner. They take turns giving definitions of the combinations and guessing the answers.

Answers
in<u>crea</u>singly <u>diff</u>icult
<u>rel</u>atively <u>sta</u>ble
sig<u>nif</u>icantly <u>diff</u>erent
unex<u>pec</u>tedly <u>ra</u>pid
po<u>ten</u>tially dis<u>as</u>trous
app<u>rec</u>iably more <u>hos</u>tile
pro<u>found</u>ly <u>worr</u>ying
irre<u>trie</u>vably <u>dam</u>aging

Exercise 7

Students decide which adverbs in **6** could be replaced by *noticeably, comparatively, considerably* and *surprisingly*, without changing the meaning.

Answers
noticeably = could replace *significantly/appreciably*
comparatively = could replace *relatively*
considerably = could replace *significantly/appreciably*
surprisingly = could replace *unexpectedly*

Further practice

If students need more practice, go to *Practice file 11* on page 122 of the *Student's Book*.

Exercise 8

Students rewrite statements 1–7 using the adverbs in brackets and an appropriate adjective, so the meaning remains the same. They can then compare answers with a partner.

Suggested answers
1 The reduction in our share value is profoundly concerning.
2 The number of people leaving the company this year is comparatively low.
3 Last year's share-dealing scandal has been irretrievably damaging to the company's reputation.
4 Recruiting well-qualified people is becoming increasingly difficult.
5 The change in market conditions has been surprisingly quick.
6 Don't forget that in many respects our cultures are considerably different.
7 Their attitude towards us is noticeably less friendly.

Exercise 9

Students work with a partner. Student A turns to the information on page 142 of the *Student's Book* and Student B turns to page 137. Allow time for them to read the information and prepare their explanation. They then take turns to explain the situations using vocabulary from **6** and **7**. Before they read, you might want to check that students understand the following:
abide by = to accept and act according to a law or a rule
robust = strong; able to survive; being used a lot and not likely to break

EXTENSION Ask students to write a formal email from the head of PR to senior managers in the company they focused on in **9**, summarizing the situation.

Exercise 10

Students work with a partner and prepare a statement. Remind them to focus on what's important for a new employee and encourage them to use vocabulary from this section. When they are ready, ask each pair to read out their statement to the rest of the class.

When students read out their statements, divide the rest of the class into two groups. Group A should note any good use of language, or any possible errors. Group B should listen and decide if they would like to work for that company. Discuss the feedback as a class after each statement.

PRE-WORK LEARNERS Students work with a partner and choose either Company X or Company Y from **9**. Ask them to think about the core values that the company might have, based on the information on pages 137 and 142 of the *Student's Book*. Then ask them to prepare a short values statement for the company.

Photocopiable worksheet

Download and photocopy *Unit 11 Working with words worksheet* from the teacher resources in the *Online practice*.

Business communication

Exercise 1

As a lead-in to this section, ask students to think of all the cosmetics companies they know (e.g. L'Oréal, the Body Shop, Avon, Estée Lauder). Find out which products your students use and if they have had any bad experiences with any cosmetic products. Then ask students to read the *Context* about Alanas Pharma Inc. They can then read the email to find out about the problem and the possible consequences.

> **Answers**
> The problem is that the new factory in South Korea can't meet demands.
> The company won't be able to meet its deadlines. Laura and Andrew may not have enough stock for the launch in Berlin.

Exercise 2

▶ 11.2 Students listen to the first part of the conference call and then discuss the questions with a partner. Before they listen, you might want to check that students understand the following:

backlog (of work) = a quantity of work that should have been done already, but has not yet been done

pushy = trying hard to get what you want in a way that seems rude

> **Answers**
> 1 The factory has had too many orders and therefore can't meet the deadline.
> 2 Laura
> 3 If they don't have the product for the launch, the launch cannot take place. If the product launch is delayed, this may cause irreversible damage to the company's sales/reputation, etc.

Exercise 3

Students put expressions 1–7 into categories a–c.

> **Answers**
> a 4, 6
> b 2
> c 1, 3, 5, 7

Exercise 4

▶ 11.3 Students listen to the second part of the conference call and then discuss questions 1–3 with a partner.

> **Answers**
> 1 publicizing products, but supplying them to customers after the exhibition; speeding up delivery so that products arrive on the last day and then have the launch party on the last day; use a different (local) supplier; use just samples instead
> 2 Andrew is negative about all suggestions, except his own (use a different supplier). Laura is more willing to consider the other suggestions.
> 3 Students' own answers

Exercise 5

▶ 11.3 Students listen again and complete expressions 1–10. Refer students to the *Key expressions* to check their answers.

> **Answers**
> 1 out of   6 stay firm
> 2 just won't   7 make do
> 3 consider   8 possibly do
> 4 the question   9 say to doing
> 5 to budge   10 be willing

Exercise 6

Students look at the expressions in **5** and answer the questions.

> **Answers**
> a 3, 7, 9
> b 1, 2, 5, 6, 8
> c 4, 10
> d 7

Exercise 7

▶ 11.4 Students listen to the final part of the conference call and answer questions 1–2.

> **Answers**
> 1 Accepting the idea of 500 samples of each cream being sent directly to Berlin is a good compromise.
> 2 Andrew is least likely to be happy.

Exercise 8

▶ 11.4 Students listen again and note the three expressions the speakers use to agree on a solution.

> **Answers**
> 1 That sounds feasible.
> 2 Are we all agreed?
> 3 Yes, I'll go along with that.

Write the tips below, for negotiating, on the board. Ask students to work in groups and decide if they think the tips are true or false, and why. Elicit their ideas, encouraging them to give reasons.

1 *Always start high with your prices and only reduce them if necessary.*
2 *Don't allow the other person to talk much.*
3 *Express your emotions – if you feel angry, show it.*
4 *Make the first move.*

Suggested answers

1 True: this gives room for negotiation and helps both sides feel that they have benefited.
2 False: let the other person talk; you should listen – this will give you more information and allow you to react in a way that will get you what you want.
3 False: stay calm and rational throughout to convey a professional image and help you get what you want.
4 False: let the other person set the agenda and then react, e.g. if they ask you how much you will charge for a service, ask them how much they would pay – this usually means you will get a higher amount.

Exercise 9

Students work with a partner. Student A turns to page 143 of the *Student's Book,* and Student B turns to page 137. Allow time for them to read their information. Refer them to the *Key expressions* and encourage them to think of arguments to support their position. When they are ready, ask them to discuss the situation and find a solution.

Monitor and give feedback on the use of language from the *Key expressions*. After their discussions, ask each pair to tell the class who benefited most from their solution and why.

Further practice

If students need more practice, go to *Practice file 11* on page 122 of the *Student's Book.*

Exercise 10

Students work with a partner. Ask them first to think of a problem or a change they'd like to make at work. They follow steps 1–3. They should discuss their ideas and make notes on how to present their proposal. They then swap their notes with another pair, read those notes, and think about their objections to the other pair's proposal.

ONE-TO-ONE Ask the student to think about their own company and a problem or change he/she would like to make at work. He/she can use the list in **10** or suggest an idea of his/her own. Ask the student to follow the steps:

1 The student decides on and then makes brief notes on the proposal he/she wants to present, including what the effects will be on the company/department.
2 The student then presents his/her proposal to you. While you listen, think of some objections to the proposal so that the student has to negotiate with you. Try to come up with a workable solution.

PRE-WORK LEARNERS Write the following changes on the board. Ask pairs to choose one of them or to come up with their own idea. They should then prepare their proposal, thinking about how the change would affect students/teachers.

• *All subjects will be taught in English.*
• *One-to-one lessons will be introduced and every student should have one per week.*
• *Students will negotiate every syllabus with the teacher in the first lesson.*

Exercise 11

Pairs join to form groups of four. They then discuss each proposal and negotiate a solution.

CULTURE QUESTION Students can discuss the questions in pairs before sharing their answers with the rest of the class. Answers will vary, but discussions may focus on the fact that in some cultures group harmony takes precedence over individual performance and therefore the negotiating style is likely to be influenced by this. These cultures are referred to as 'collectivist' for example, Japan, China, Korea, Taiwan, Argentina, Brazil and India.

Photocopiable worksheet

Download and photocopy *Unit 11 Business communication worksheet* from the teacher resources in the *Online practice*.

Language at work

Exercise 1

Students match the participle phrases in italics in 1–6 to the descriptions a–e.

Answers

a 2, 4	d 1
b 5	e 3
c 6	

Exercise 2

Students complete sentences 1–6 using the phrases from the list. Sometimes more than one answer is possible. They can then compare their answers with a partner.

Possible answers

1 Having read / Given	4 After meeting / Knowing
2 Knowing / Having read	5 Faced with / Given / Having read
3 Given	6 Offering

Exercise 3

Students compare the sentences in A and B and answer questions 1–2 with a partner.

Answers

1 Subject/verb word order changes. Inversion gives the sentences in B the same form as a question: the subject, *One of our contracts*, changes places with the auxiliary verb, *has*.
2 to emphasize something and/or make something sound more formal

Grammar reference

If students need more information, go to *Grammar Reference* on page 132 of the *Student's Book*.

Exercise 4

Students rewrite the sentences using an inversion to add emphasis or formality.

Answers
1 At no time will we be willing to compromise our customer-care policy.
2 Under no circumstances will we negotiate a new deal.
3 Not only did you ask us to cut costs, but you also asked us to reduce our lead time.

Further practice

If students need more practice, go to *Practice file 11* on page 123 of the *Student's Book*.

Exercise 5

As a lead-in, ask students the following questions:

- *What health and safety rules are there at your place of work/study?*
- *Are they sufficient?*
- *Would it be a good idea to tighten the rules? Why/Why not?*

Then ask them to work in pairs and create a formal statement, using ideas from the list or their own ideas. Ask them to include inversion where possible. When they are ready, ask each pair to make their announcement to the rest of the class.

Monitor for correct use of participle clauses and inversion and correct intonation/word stress. Give feedback where necessary.

Possible answers
1 Not only did staff take ten minutes longer than necessary to evacuate the building, but it was also clear people were ignoring the instructions to keep the fire doors closed. In the event of a fire all employees are reminded they must evacuate the building quickly and calmly using the stairs. Under no circumstances can the lifts be used once a fire alarm has gone off.
2 Having had several minor accidents on the production line, employees are reminded that they must wear the correct protective clothing at all times.
3 Under no circumstances can any employee or student drive or cycle on company premises. Given the dangers that this poses, employees breaking this rule will be disciplined.
4 Given the number of staff who have suffered back injuries while taking deliveries recently, trolleys must be used to move all heavy boxes that come into the warehouse.

PRE-WORK LEARNERS Ask students to imagine that they are the staff/management of their school or college. They should work with a partner to prepare an announcement on any health and safety regulations that students have recently been ignoring.

EXTRA ACTIVITY Students work in groups. Write the following rules/situations on the board. Tell students that they are flight attendants and they need to make three announcements to passengers about 1–3 (below). They also need to speak to one of the passengers about the situation in 4. Ask them to prepare what they would say, using inversion where possible. (Suggested answers are in brackets.)

1 *Drink lots of water and avoid drinking too much coffee and alcohol.* (Not only should you try to drink lots of water during the flight, but you should also avoid drinking too much coffee or alcohol.)
2 *No sharp instruments (e.g. knives) in hand luggage.* (Under no circumstances are sharp instruments allowed to be brought onto the plane in hand luggage.)
3 *No smoking.* (At no time are you permitted to smoke during the flight.)
4 *Situation = a passenger with medication was not allowed to take it onto the plane because he didn't show you a letter from his doctor. He is now complaining about this.* (Had I seen your letter from the doctor, I would have allowed you to bring your medication on board.)

Photocopiable worksheet

Download and photocopy *Unit 11 Language at work worksheet* from the teacher resources in the *Online practice*.

Practically speaking

Exercise 1

▶ 11.5 As a lead-in, dictate or write the following situations and questions on the board. Ask students to discuss them in pairs.

- *Shared an office with a noisy/untidy colleague*
- *Had a colleague who was always late for meetings with you*
- *Received bad quality work from a colleague*
1 *Have you experienced any of these situations?*
2 *Did you say anything about it to the person involved? If you did, what did you say and was it effective? If not, why not and what happened?*

Students then listen and answer the questions.

Answers
1 Extract 1: She speaks very loudly on the phone.
   Extract 2: He must dress more smartly for the situation that's coming up.
   Extract 3: The report isn't good enough.
   Extract 4: She is not happy with the package that goes with the new job (i.e. salary, etc.).
   Extract 5: They haven't given enough information.
2 In all extracts, the person raising the point sounds apologetic and respectful, and is quite careful with their choice of words. The other people respond in different ways: in 1, she is understanding and apologetic; in 2, he is a bit offended and rather defensive; in 3, she is a bit upset; in 4, they seem open to discussion; in 5, he is very defensive.

Exercise 2

▶ **11.5** Students listen again and complete sentences 1–5.

Answers
1 I don't mean to sound rude
2 this is a bit delicate / don't take offence
3 please don't take this the wrong way / the thing is
4 quite sure how to put this
5 respect / I have to say that / The fact is

Exercise 3

Students read statements 1–5 and rewrite them using phrases from **2** to make them less direct.

Possible answers
1 Look, this is a bit delicate. Please don't take offence, but I'm afraid your design isn't very good. I was thinking I could ask someone else to do it instead. What do you think?
2 I'm sorry, I don't mean to sound rude, but do you think you could try to control your laugh a bit? It's a bit loud, and it might be disturbing some of the others.
3 Listen, we'd be delighted if you took on this job, don't get us wrong. But, you see, the thing is, I have to say that the price really does seem rather high. I'm afraid we just wouldn't be able to pay quite that much.
4 Oh, have you got a minute? Well, you see, the thing is, I know you've put in an awful lot of effort and have really tried hard. But, well, it's just that over the last year your performance hasn't really improved very much. And it's got to the point that we won't be able to give you an increase in pay until there are some significant improvements.
5 I don't mean to sound rude but, well, I was wondering if I could ask you not to leave dirty mugs around? Do you think you could put them in the kitchen, and perhaps even wash them up?

EXTENSION Ask students to work in pairs and to look at their rewritten sentences in **3**. They should think of a suitable response to each one (see possible ideas below). Then ask them to practise the conversations using these ideas:

1 Well, actually, I'd rather have another go. May I? / Sure. Who do you have in mind? / Oh, really. What exactly don't you like about it?
2 I'm sorry. I didn't realize. / I have got quite a loud laugh. Sorry. / Oh, it's this really funny email. I'll forward it to you.
3 How much can you pay? / Well, then I'm sorry. We can't do it.
4 What specifically do I need to do? / That's strange. I've been getting really positive feedback recently.
5 Oh, sure. Sorry. / Well, actually, they're not mine. / I suppose so. Is someone else going to throw away the pizza boxes?

Useful phrases

Refer students to the *Useful phrases* section on page 136 of the *Student's Book* for extension and revision.

Exercise 4

Students work with a partner and read the situations. They then have a conversation about one of the situations, taking turns to raise the difficult points. The other student should respond appropriately.

Monitor students' use of language. You should also check that they're using polite intonation. Provide feedback at the end of the task.

ONE-TO-ONE Ask the student to raise the difficult points in three of the situations and you raise one of the difficult points to give him/her practice in responding to a difficult point.

After you have done the exercise, ask the student how he/she felt as the person raising the point and the person receiving the complaint.

KEY WORD
Students read the phrases and match each to the appropriate definition.

Answers
1 e 2 c 3 a 4 d 5 b

Progress test

Download and photocopy *Unit 11 Progress test* and *Speaking test* from the teacher resources in the *Online practice*.

Talking point

Discussion

Exercise 1

Students read the *Context* and the article and answer the question. Be prepared to answer any questions they may have about vocabulary. They can discuss their ideas with a partner.

Possible answer
It could be that whistle-blowing is considered disloyal in traditional Japanese business practices.

EXTENSION You could ask students what they think about whistle-blowers. Is it a good thing to do? Who does it benefit? What possible reasons are there for whistle-blowing? Can they think of a case they have read or heard about?

You could ask them to find out about famous whistle-blowers online and then tell the rest of the class about what they found out.

Exercise 2

Students discuss their ideas with a partner.

Exercise 3

Students look at the table and discuss their ideas with a partner. If students do not know much about either culture, you could ask them to find out by checking on the Internet. They could discuss whether cultural values in their country or company are more similar to those in the UK or in Japan.

Exercise 4

Once students have decided on the cultural values in both countries, they decide what Michael Woodford could have done differently. They can also decide what they might have done in the same situation. Do they think the result would have been the same?

PRE-WORK LEARNERS Ask students in what circumstances they would feel they had to do what Michael Woodford did. What do they think the consequences might be?

You could ask them to find examples in the news of scandals and whistle-blowing, and what happened to the employee and the company after the scandal broke.

Task

Exercise 1

As a lead-in, ask students to think about what the expected standards, values, beliefs and ways of behaving in their company are. With a partner, students list what they would expect to read in a 'Code of Conduct' or be told in 'Compliance Training' sessions. They can then think of the questions they expect to be asked.

Exercise 2

Students work with a partner. If they work in the same company, they can prepare the main points to discuss in a meeting to agree on five values for their company and write the framework for the company's Code of Conduct. If students work in different companies, they can make up an imaginary company. They write the framework for the imaginary company, preparing the main points to discuss in the meeting. Be ready to help with vocabulary where necessary.

PRE-WORK LEARNERS Ask students to work with a partner. They choose a well-known company and find out about the company Code of Conduct and values online. They then write the framework of the company they have chosen.

Exercise 3

Students now work in groups of four and have the meeting. Refer them to phrases for raising difficult points in *Practically speaking* on page 91 and for reaching an agreement in *Business communication* on page 89 if they need more support. When the meeting is finished, they should work together to complete the notes.

Each group presents and justifies its decisions to the rest of the class. Ask students to comment on how their group presented and justified their ideas. Did they give reasons for their decisions? Were the values expressed closer to British or Japanese values?

ONE-TO-ONE Ask the student to read the information in the *Context* and the article and then go through the questions in the *Discussion* together. In the *Task* the student writes a framework for his/her company and presents it to you.

EXTENSION Ask students to write a report on the meeting for their manager. The report can have three sections:

1 Company values: They should set out the five values clearly.
2 The Code of Conduct: They outline the main points of the Code of Conduct.
3 Ways of checking acceptance and understanding: They set out the ways that acceptance and understanding of the Code will be checked, making sure each way can be clearly understood by the company staff.

12 Persuasion

Unit content

By the end of this unit, students will be able to
- discuss persuasion
- sell an idea using discourse markers
- deal with compliments.

Context

Over two thousand years ago, the Greek philosopher, Aristotle, defined *Persuasion* as the ability to convince others to adopt your ideas. Today, it's an increasingly important concept, and one your students will relate to on several levels. As consumers, they will be constantly subjected to persuasive messages through advertising. They are also likely to have observed politicians using highly-refined persuasive techniques. They will have had to use persuasive techniques themselves, both in their working lives and in their personal relationships. They may have had to sell their company's service/products to customers, and may have even been involved in developing persuasive publicity for their company.

Effective persuasive techniques are becoming more and more important in the business world, for both individuals and for companies. A person's powers of persuasion can often contribute directly to their ability to achieve goals. Someone with strong persuasive techniques can speak logically, fluently and confidently, and if they are effective, they are convincing and trustworthy, and understand the needs and motivations of others. This makes it far easier for them to get what they want out of a situation.

The first part of this unit looks at persuasion in advertising, and how techniques vary according to the culture of the target market. Students then focus on the language for selling an idea and how to use spoken discourse markers to punctuate their speech. They also give and respond to compliments. In the *Viewpoint* video they watch interviews which look at the differences between leadership and management, as perceived in the past and present and how they are likely to change in the future.

Starting point

As a lead-in, ask students to brainstorm a list of decisions they have to make (both in their personal lives and their working lives), e.g. where to go on holiday, buying a car, buying gadgets, buying clothes, voting, where to advertise, office location, etc. Write their ideas on the board. Students can then work with a partner to discuss the questions, before sharing their answers with the rest of the class.

EXTENSION Write the following words on the board:

- *children*
- *teenagers*
- *adults*
- *old people*

Then write the following questions on the board and ask students to discuss them with a partner.

- *Which of these groups would be most easily persuaded/ influenced? Why?*
- *Which age group would be the hardest to persuade/ influence? Why?*
- *Does a person's personality affect how easily they are persuaded? Why? Give examples.*
- *Does the amount of money a person has affect how easily they are persuaded/influenced? Give examples.*

Working with words

Exercise 1

As a lead-in, elicit different kinds of advertising, e.g. social media, pop-ups on websites, word-of-mouth, posters, magazine/TV commercials, etc. Students could think of one advertisement that is successful and decide why it is. Students then work with a partner and discuss the question, before reading the text to compare their answers. Before they read, you might want to check that students understand *conform* (to behave and think in the same way as most other people in a group or society).

> **Answers**
> Advertisers generate demand for products/services using images and messages. They exploit consumers' desires to belong and to gain social status.

Exercise 2

Students work with a partner and think of examples of adverts for each category. They can then discuss their examples as a class.

> **Possible answers**
> Need: bottled water (in many countries), exercise gadgets
> Belonging: fashion, make-up
> Esteem: cars, exotic holidays

Exercise 3

Students match phrases 1–13 with definitions a–m.

Answers
1 b 2 d 3 a 4 c 5 f 6 e 7 i 8 l 9 k 10 j
11 g 12 m 13 h

PRONUNCIATION Write the two phrases below on the board and ask students to identify any weak forms, i.e. schwas /ə/ (see underlined sections for the answers). Note that the final prepositions in these phrases (*to, for*) will be weak when used in full sentences.

- *reinforce an association between*
- *tailor something towards a need*

Then ask students to look at the other phrases in **3**. They should work in pairs and underline the weak forms in these phrases.

Answers

promote consumption of	be taken in by
generate a demand for	buy into
hold out for	pick up on
appeal to	put across
live up to	tap into
play on emotions	

Exercise 4

Students work with a partner and look at the advertisements. They then use the phrases from **3** to discuss what each is trying to achieve.

Suggested answers
1 appeals to adults wanting a tempting dessert; taps into concerns about health; also humorous slogan that allows people to do something they perhaps shouldn't
2 appeals to young men; generates the demand for fashionable clothes, and taps into the fear of being left out
3 appeals to adults who wish to be seen as different and wanting to stand out in a crowd; also the photo gives the idea of being somewhat unconventional and unpredictable

ALTERNATIVE If students find this difficult, write the following phrases on the board:

- *This is trying to …*
- *This image is aiming to …*
- *I think an advert like this would …*

Then ask them to look at the advertisements and to try to complete the sentences.

EXTENSION Bring in a selection of magazine adverts (or ask students to bring them) to the next lesson. Give each pair one advert to discuss.(They shouldn't show them to any other students.) When they're ready, collect all the adverts/pictures, and stick them up around the room. Pairs then take turns to explain the message behind their advert to the rest of the class without saying which product it is. The others have to guess.

Exercise 5

▶ 12.1 Students listen to the interview and answer questions 1–3. Before they listen, you might want to check that students understand the following:
aspirational = wanting to achieve success in your career, and/or to improve your social status and standard of living
an imperative = a thing that is very important and needs immediate attention or action
to get on = to be successful in your career
to keep up with = to move, make progress or increase at the same rate as somebody/something else

Answers
1 Because Americans are very competitive, advertisers have to focus on persuading customers about how they will benefit from the product in terms of health, social status, youthfulness, etc.
2 Denmark is less competitive, and Danes are far less materialistic and showy than Americans, therefore fewer luxury items are sold. Russia and China haven't had the choice of many products until recently, so advertisers focus more on pointing out the main product facts and features.
3 Students' own answers

EXTRA ACTIVITY
Ask students to work with a partner and discuss what could be said about advertising in their culture(s). They should then share their ideas with the rest of the class.

EXTENSION Find out from your students what adverts are currently popular or high profile in their country. Write a list of examples from students on the board. Then ask students to describe their reactions to them. Do they think these adverts would be effective in Russia, China, Denmark or the US?

Exercise 6

Students complete comments 1–8 using words from the list. You might want to check that students understand the following term:
USP = Unique Selling Proposition / Point – a statement that identifies what makes a person, product or organization different from or better than its competitors.

Answers

1	exploitative	5	motivational
2	USP	6	status anxiety
3	aspirational	7	market penetration
4	materialistic	8	consumer profile

Draw the table below on the board. Ask students to copy it into their notebooks. They should then complete the table with a partner. Ask them to identify the word stress (underlined).

Verb	Noun	Adjective
		exploitative
		motivational
		aspirational

When students have checked their answers as a class, ask them to work with a partner and formulate sentences using the words. Note that the noun *exploit* (a brave, exciting or interesting act), often used in the plural, is very different from *exploitation* (a situation in which somebody treats somebody else in an unfair way, especially in order to make money from their work).

Answers

Verb	Noun	Adjective
ex<u>ploit</u>	exploi<u>ta</u>tion	ex<u>ploi</u>tative
	<u>ex</u>ploit(s)	
<u>mo</u>tivate	moti<u>va</u>tion	moti<u>va</u>tional
a<u>spire</u> (to)	aspi<u>ra</u>tion	aspi<u>ra</u>tional

Further practice

If students need more practice, go to *Practice file 12* on page 124 of the *Student's Book*.

Exercise 7

Students work with a partner and discuss the questions. Allow the discussion to flow freely. Give positive feedback to students who make effective use of the vocabulary from this section.

Students can describe a company they know well. Alternatively, ask students to do some research for the next lesson. They should choose one company, and find out how it markets itself. Does it have different adverts in different countries? Ask them to bring examples to the next lesson, and to be prepared to talk briefly about what they found.

Photocopiable worksheet

Download and photocopy *Unit 12 Working with words worksheet* from the teacher resources in the *Online practice*.

Business communication

Exercise 1

Students work with a partner and discuss questions 1–2.

Possible answers
1 reach a wider customer base; keep products up-to-date; keep customers happy; maintain success
2 very, otherwise they won't be willing to make them work

Exercise 2

▶ **12.2**–**12.5** Students read the *Context* about Ranjit Shetty. Then they listen to the four extracts from the presentation and answer questions 1–4. Before they listen, you might want to check that students understand the following:
ring alarm bells = to cause people to start to feel worried and suspicious
brutally = violently and cruelly
solely = only; not involving somebody/something else
guru = a person who is an expert on a particular subject or who is very good at doing something

Answers
1 In the long term the business will dry up and the company might go bankrupt.
2 More companies invest in multimedia advertising now than in print advertising. This will also help them gain new customers and get a higher position in the market.
3 He has appointed an in-house specialist and his assistant will take over his work. They have external investment for the plan and have employed an outside consultant.
4 because they are acting ahead of time

Exercise 3

▶ **12.2**–**12.5** Students listen to the four extracts again and answer questions 1–2. They can then compare their answers in pairs before sharing answers with the rest of the class.

Answers
1 assertive, upbeat, enthusiastic
2 invites audience members to speak; uses rhetorical questions; addresses the audience directly; uses word stress and intonation; shocks the audience (when talking about the competition); uses visuals; keeps a fast pace; uses tripling (lists of three points – *We're committed …*, *we're motivated …*, *and we believe in what we do …*); uses positive language/ vocabulary; speaks with enthusiasm

Exercise 4

Students match categories 1–5 to explanations a–e. You might want to check that students understand *on board* (working together). If it helps, you could use an image of a ship, where all passengers are on the ship / on board, going somewhere together, to help students to remember the meaning.

Answers
1 b **2** d **3** a **4** e **5** c

Exercise 5

Students match expressions a–j with categories 1–5 in **4**. Refer students to the *Key expressions* box to check their answers.

Answers
a 5 **b** 2 **c** 1 **d** 3 **e** 3 **f** 5 **g** 2 **h** 1 **i** 4 **j** 4

Exercise 6

Students work with a partner. They look at the slides and decide which expressions from the *Key expressions* could be used. They then take turns to give the presentation.

Further practice

If students need more practice, go to *Practice file 12* on page 124 of the *Student's Book*.

Exercise 7

Students work with a partner. Give them time to think of an idea and to prepare a presentation to convince the rest of the class. Encourage students to think about why the idea is a good one and how they will support their argument (e.g. how colleagues will benefit). They should also be ready to show awareness of any problems it may cause, and try to get their audience's commitment. Refer them to the *Key expressions* during the preparation stage.

Ask the class to give feedback after each presentation. They should think about answers to the following questions:

- Was the presentation effective?
- Did they convince the audience that it's a good idea?

PRE-WORK LEARNERS If your students have no work experience, they can base their ideas on a company they know well. Alternatively, they can develop an idea for where they study. If they are finding it difficult to think of an idea, write the following examples on the board:

- *Introduce a one-semester exchange programme with a British / American / Australian college or university.*
- *Start a mentoring system: older students have one-to-one sessions with newer students to help them with their learning and with managing their workload.*

EXTENSION If possible, record the presentations and listen/watch the recording before giving feedback.

Photocopiable worksheet

Download and photocopy *Unit 12 Business communication worksheet* from the teacher resources in the *Online practice*.

Language at work

Exercise 1

▶ 12.6 The focus here is on discourse markers (words and short phrases to help clarify the speaker's message, and to give signposts to the listener). They are used structurally to give clarity to information, and can be considered as 'lexical grammar' items. They are very common in native-speaker English and using them effectively will increase the fluency of learners at this level. Before they listen, ask students to look at the sentences. Can they think of any phrases that go in the gaps? Students then listen and complete the sentences.

Exercise 2

Students categorize the discourse markers in **1** to categories a–e. Remind students that the discourse markers may have more than one function.

PRONUNCIATION To help students use discourse markers effectively, write the following phrases on the board and ask students to identify which words or parts of words are stressed (answers are underlined).

to tell you the <u>truth</u>

after <u>all</u>

ad<u>mitt</u>edly

Then ask students to listen to all the sentences in **1** again (audio 12.6) and to mark the stress.

EXTENSION Ask students to work in pairs and to think of other discourse markers to add to each category in **2**. Then ask pairs to share their ideas with the rest of the class.

Grammar reference

If students need more information, go to *Grammar reference* on page 133 of the *Student's Book*.

Exercise 3

Students work individually and complete the extract with discourse markers from **1**, using the information in brackets to help them. They can compare answers with a partner.

Possible answers

1	Quite honestly	7	as I was saying
2	Admittedly	8	As a matter of fact
3	Obviously	9	Mind you
4	Of course	10	Anyway
5	after all	11	so to speak
6	basically	12	to tell you the truth

Further practice

If students need more practice, go to *Practice file 12* on page 125 of the *Student's Book*.

Exercise 4

Students work individually at first. They should choose one category of news, and prepare to talk about it. They should then work with their partner and describe the news using appropriate discourse markers.

Monitor and make sure they use the discourse markers in **1** appropriately.

> **EXTRA ACTIVITY**
>
> For homework ask students to find a short news item in a newspaper or business magazine. They should prepare to talk about it in class next time, explaining their reaction to it and giving their opinion. Encourage them to use discourse markers naturally when doing so.

Photocopiable worksheet

Download and photocopy *Unit 12 Language at work worksheet* from the teacher resources in the *Online practice*.

Practically speaking

This section deals with compliments. If you have students from cultures where this can be a sensitive issue, approach it with caution.

Exercise 1

▶ **12.7** As a lead-in, ask students if they have complimented anyone, or been complimented by anyone today, or in the past few days. If so, what was the compliment about? What was said? Then ask students to listen to six conversations and answer questions a–c.

Answers
a 2, 3, 6
b 1, 4, 5
c 3, 4, 6

Exercise 2

▶ **12.7** Students listen again and answer the question.

Answers
In extract 3 the compliment is fine, but the response is not appropriate; it could sound boastful, as she obviously has enough money to afford expensive shoes.
In extract 4 the compliment is rather strong, so it might have caused embarrassment.
In extract 6 the compliment is inappropriate.

Exercise 3

Students decide which of the phrases 1–15 are used to compliment someone (C) and which are a response (R).

Answers
compliments: 1, 2, 5, 6, 7, 8, 11, 12, 14, 15*
responses: 3, 4, 9, 10, 13
*Note that 15 (*you have very nice …*) could often be inappropriate, so warn students to avoid using this phrase unless they are certain it won't cause offence.

Useful phrases

Refer students to the *Useful phrases* section on page 136 of the *Student's Book* for extension and revision.

Exercise 4

Students work with a partner. They take turns to compliment each other, using phrases from **3**. Remind them to be careful to avoid making their partner feel uncomfortable and to respond to compliments appropriately.

> **EXTRA ACTIVITY**
>
> Give each student three slips of paper. They should write down three topics that someone could be complimented on, each on a different piece of paper. Encourage them to make the compliments interesting, but not embarrassing, e.g. clothing, a new haircut, a presentation, participation in a meeting, a new brochure, etc.
>
> Ask them to swap their papers with another student. Ask students to mingle and find another student to talk to – they should choose one of the compliment topics, give the compliment and hand over the corresponding piece of paper. They will then receive a compliment and should respond appropriately. Each student will now have two of their original pieces of paper, plus another topic that they can then use with other students.
>
> Allow the activity to continue for a few minutes. Then ask students to return to their seats. Ask the class how they felt during the activity. Were there any awkward moments? Why?

> **CULTURE QUESTION**
>
> Students can discuss these questions in small groups. Answers will vary, although the following issues may arise. It is safe in most cultures to comment generally on someone's well-being. It's usually best to avoid commenting on specific parts of the body (especially to women), e.g. eyes, smile, legs, hands, etc. In some cultures, people find it difficult to accept compliments (they make them feel uncomfortable). In Arabic cultures, commenting positively on a possession can prompt the host to give you that possession.

> **KEY WORD**
>
> Students match the use of *kill* in phrases 1–6 to definitions a–f.
>
> ### Answers
> 1 e   2 a   3 d   4 b   5 c   6 f

Progress test

Download and photocopy *Unit 12 Progress test* and *Speaking test* from the teacher resources in the *Online practice*.

Viewpoint 4

Exercise 1

Students work with a partner. They read 12 different descriptions of ways of doing things in business and decide if they refer to business practices in the past, present or future.

Possible answers

Answers will vary, particularly in different countries where there are different styles of management and leadership, but in the UK these are possible answers:
Past: 3, 4, 5, 9, 10 (in an ideal world)
Present: 1, 6, 11, 12
Future: 2, 7, 8

Exercise 2

Students work in small groups. They compare and discuss the reasons for their answers in **1**. They then think of three more descriptions they can categorize in the past, present and future.

Exercise 3

Before students watch the video, they match the words and phrases 1–10 from the interview to definitions a–j. They can compare their answers with a partner.

Answers

1 d **2** g **3** b **4** e **5** a **6** c **7** f **8** j **9** h **10** i

Exercise 4

▶ 01 Students watch Professor Tim Morris answering three different questions and number the questions A–C in the order he answers them.

In his answers Tim Morris uses lots of good discourse markers – you can make students aware of these. It might be helpful for students to either read the subtitles on the video, or for you to write two or three sentences from the script on the board and ask students to read them out loud to get a feel for the use and rhythm. Example sentences showing possible breaks, stressed words (underlined) and discourse markers (in italics) for reading out loud are:

'There's a <u>vast</u> <u>amount</u> of <u>research</u> that shows that if you want to produce a <u>successful</u> <u>change</u> <u>process</u> and you want to produce <u>beneficial</u> <u>outcomes</u>, then <u>basically</u> you need to <u>engage</u> your staff in the <u>process</u> of <u>change</u>.'

'It's <u>perfectly</u> <u>viable</u> to draw <u>boundaries</u> round things, but staff <u>do</u> <u>need</u> to have some <u>understanding</u> of what's going on and to be <u>engaged</u> in various ways – <u>maybe</u> to offer <u>perspectives</u> that <u>haven't</u> been understood before, but also to *actually* <u>help</u> the process along.'

Answers

A 2 **B** 1 **C** 3

Exercise 5

▶ 02 Before students watch the video, ask them if they remember how they defined the difference between a leader and a manager in *Unit 10*. They watch the first part of the interview again. Working with a partner, they decide which aspects were associated with leaders (L) or managers (M) in the past.

Answers

vision L
making things work effectively M
running systems M
monitoring M
long-term strategy L
change L
continuity M
managing the organization's environment L
innovation L

Exercise 6

Ask students to decide why Professor Tim Morris thinks these past ideas about leadership and management are false. Ask them to give reasons for their answers.

Answers

Tim Morris thinks these ideas about leadership and management are false because anyone who is managing people is leading them, and also has to give a sense of direction and engage with people so that they want to follow.

Exercise 7

▶ 03 Students watch the second part of the interview and decide if Professor Morris thinks the statements are true (T) or false (F). Tell students to note down any words or phrases he uses that support their answers.

Answers
1 F – ... it's not like you can say, well, people start to emerge when they're 27 or 33.
2 T – ... what I would say is that we normally don't put people into leadership positions of any substance, usually until they're in their 30s. / ... what I would tend to assume is that between say the ages of early 30s through to say mid-40s, that's when leadership development is ... is taking place very intensively
3 T – ... what you can find is, first of all, in particular with the emphasis on entrepreneurial organizations and people starting businesses, or being thrown into the, sort of, deep end much earlier in their lives. It's not uncommon for people to be really picking up, sort of, their first leadership challenge, formally or informally, in their mid-20s
4 F – ... I've certainly worked with people who, you know, only in their 40s, maybe even their 50s, really have grasped the nettle in terms of saying, well, I want to be a leader – I can lead others. They're what you might call (as) late developers or they're people who've never had the chance and the opportunity or thought themselves capable.
5 T – ... more and more women have come back to work after they've had families, and they've got what we call second careers or second career – second parts of their career. And they're coming back having had some time out so they're a bit older and so on, and wiser, and it's then that they take up the leadership challenge.
6 T – ... I think the lesson is basically, don't think you're ever too old, as it were, or too young to be a leader.

Exercise 8

▶ 04 Students watch the third part of the interview about how to learn leadership and make notes about the three areas and why they are important. They compare and discuss their answers with a partner.

Answers
Experience: Tim Morris thinks you can't learn from books, you need to do it.
Formal learning: Some leadership skills can be taught, for example, on MBA programmes.
Self-reflection: When you reflect you can see what you do well, and what you need to change. It stops you staying in the same style, in a rut, and helps you think of different ways to do things.

Exercise 9

With a partner, students discuss questions 1–3. They can then report back their ideas to the class. Encourage students to use the words and phrases in **3** and the language from the interview.

Give positive feedback on the use of language and write any mistakes on the board for the class to correct.

PRE-WORK LEARNERS Encourage students with minimal or no work experience to talk about their experience of leaders and leadership styles in teams outside work/study places, e.g. teams in sports, music, clubs, etc.

Exercise 10

▶ 05 Ask students to read questions 1–7 carefully before they watch the video. They watch and make notes to answer the questions. Don't check the answers at this stage.

Exercise 11

▶ 05 Students work in small groups and compare their notes from **10**. They can then watch the video again to check their answers and add details to their notes.

Answers
1 He says that people thought people were born with leadership traits. If you didn't have them, you couldn't be a leader, but if you did then you'd become a leader whatever the situation.
2 charisma
3 nonsense – He believes everybody has the capacity for leadership.
4 It will impact on every aspect of how we do business; every aspect of how we organize; every aspect of how we interact and come together to produce something more than any one individual can.
5 He thinks we should see it as a set of behaviours and a set of skills, but also a set of roles.
6 In the future, all of us will be required to be capable of analysing and scanning our environment, of influencing others to do something different from what they might otherwise choose to do, of acting as a figure-head of political brokering, of allocating resources, of motivating.
7 We should see work as something intrinsic to our own personal purpose and fulfilment.

Exercise 12

Students work in groups to prepare a one-day course entitled 'Managing and leading the future'. The day includes four workshops on different topics. The group decides on the name of each session and then lists the main points of each one. They then prepare a short presentation on their course for the rest of the class.

Exercise 13

Students present and compare their training schedules. The class can decide which sessions they think are most useful and come up with a class training schedule.

ONE-TO-ONE Ask the student to design the four sessions on a one-day course that would benefit his/her company and present them to you. He/she gives the aims of each session and explains why it would be useful.

Further ideas and video scripts

You can find a list of suggested ideas for how to use video in the class in the teacher resources in the *Online practice*. The video scripts are available to download from the Teaching Resources on the Oxford Teachers' Club. www.oup.com/elt/teacher/businessresult

Practice file answer key

Unit 1

Working with words

Exercise 1
1	read	7	form
2	build	8	gave
3	weighed up	9	build
4	processed	10	work
5	keep	11	managing
6	take	12	kept

Exercise 2
1	down to earth	7	an easy-going
2	out-of-the-way	8	time-consuming
3	outspoken	9	open-minded
4	low-key	10	self-assured
5	run-of-the-mill	11	up-and-coming
6	unexpected	12	tedious

Business communication

Exercise 1
1	convinced	6	anything
2	anticipated	7	've got to
3	wouldn't	8	confident
4	I'm not saying	9	a reason
5	wary	10	can't

Exercise 2
1 I'm **just not** 100% convinced
2 I'm **absolutely / quite** sure that
3 To be **fair / honest**, the whole matter
4 I **gathered** from your report
5 I wouldn't go **so far / as far** as to say
6 From **what** I could see

Exercise 3
Suggested answers only
1 From what I could see, the meeting went much better than we expected.
2 I'm not saying the trip didn't go well – it's just that there were some problems.
3 I've got to say / I'm fully confident that the proposed site would be perfect for the company.
4 According to Fred / I gathered from Fred that the project is going fairly well.

Language at work

Exercise 1
1	are growing, has made	3	reflects, have continued
2	have expanded, have been	4	takes, is stepping

Exercise 2
1 We will have completed …
2 We had originally hoped …
3 … who have been working on it …
4 I'll be taking … / I'll take …
5 … there seems to be …
6 We're going to send … / We'll be sending … / We're sending … / We'll send …
7 I'm now handing over …, She has been working …
8 Our sales had been levelling off / had levelled off …
9 … I was thinking about this …

Unit 2

Working with words

Exercise 1
1 g	2 d	3 a	4 j	5 b
6 e	7 h	8 i	9 c	10 f

Exercise 2
1 propel yourself forward
2 stand out from (the crowd)
3 keep in with (your colleagues)
4 stand up for (your plan)
5 be burnt out from (stress)
6 play the part of (a good listener)
7 stay ahead of (the competition)
8 stand up to (analysis)
9 come up with (solutions)
10 get out there (and ask …)

Exercise 3
1	take	5	grow
2	move	6	goes
3	follow	7	put
4	Broadening	8	reach

Business communication

Exercise 1
1	get	6	come back
2	talk	7	suppose, think
3	like	8	keen on
4	mention	9	come in
5	understand	10	get on to

Exercise 2
a	2
b	7
c	1, 6, 10
d	3, 8
e	5
f	4, 9

Exercise 3
1 **Do** you want to … / Would you **like** to …
2 The obvious solution to this problem **must / would** be …
3 The **purpose** of today's meeting …
4 It's interesting you **said / say** that …
5 Could I **just** say something?
6 I'm not sure **what** your feelings are about …
7 But what makes you so **sure** …
8 Given that Arturo **doesn't** have …

Exercise 4
a	1	d	6
b	4, 7, 8	e	2
c	3	f	5

Language at work

Exercise 1
1 c	2 h	3 e	4 b	5 g
6 j	7 a	8 d	9 i	10 f

Exercise 2
1 Even if I had asked for a pay rise, I wouldn't have got one.
2 If the company had renewed our season ticket, I could have gone to the football game.
3 If only they hadn't got rid of the air-conditioning, the office wouldn't be so unbearably hot.
4 If the airport staff hadn't called off their strike yesterday, I wouldn't be in Spain now.

Exercise 3
1	should	6	have
2	might	7	had
3	would	8	might
4	have, had	9	would
5	should	10	should

Unit 3

Working with words

Exercise 1
1 efficient
2 entering, access
3 option
4 transformed
5 carried out
6 process, procedures
7 means
8 purpose
9 energetic, dynamic
10 installed

Exercise 2

1 confirmation
2 objections
3 ideas
4 performance
5 productivity
6 objections
7 development
8 difficulties

Exercise 3

1 measure the performance
2 exchange ideas
3 anticipate objections
4 facilitate productivity
5 assess the situation
6 accommodate the needs
7 generate enthusiasm
8 achieve good results

Business communication

Exercise 1

1 Just to fill you
2 something to think about
3 I'd like to start
4 put it another way
5 I mean
6 moving on
7 for example
8 turning to
9 I said earlier
10 This is where
11 Just to digress
12 And this brings me

Exercise 2

1 I've divided my talk up into …
2 First of all I'll … After that I'll …
3 I'll say more about that in a moment.
4 Just to fill you in on some of the background …
5 Now I don't know if you're familiar with …
6 And this is my key point.
7 I'll be happy to take any questions now.

Language at work

Exercise 1

(other forms are possible, but these are the best)
1 'll call
2 'll be rolling
3 'll give
4 'll have been listening, 'll take
5 'll learn
6 will have spoken
7 will yield / should yield
8 might / could / would be worth

Exercise 2

1 The consultants will probably suggest merging the departments.
2 They'll almost certainly deliver the stock in time.
3 The management are bound to ask our opinion before making the changes.
4 It's probable that the tax changes will turn investors away.
5 I've got to go now, but there's a good chance I'll see you at the launch party later.
6 The training course is unlikely to be useful. / It's unlikely that the training course will be useful.
7 The CEO is expected to make an announcement at the dinner. / It's expected that the CEO will make an announcement at the dinner.
8 They'll perhaps need more identification than a credit card. / Perhaps they'll need more identification than a credit card.

Unit 4

Working with words

Exercise 1

1 d 2 i 3 a 4 f 5 h 6 c 7 e
8 b 9 g 10 j

Exercise 2

1 reckless
2 over-cautious
3 prudent
4 rash
5 cautious
6 bold
7 foolhardy
8 risk-averse
Hidden word = sensible

Business communication

Exercise 1

1 e 2 h 3 f 4 c 5 a 6 i 7 g
8 b 9 d

Exercise 2

1 let
2 left
3 thoughts
4 respect
5 is getting
6 to sum up
7 reservations
8 in
9 draw

Language at work

Exercise 1

(Other answers are possible, but these are the best.)
1 Yes, that was one of the most useful conferences I've been to.
2 It / That should be very helpful, I think.
3 That would be disastrous.
4 It's / That's just good business practice.
5 This is / That's what's worrying me.
6 That's my problem too.

Exercise 2

1 That / It 2 That / This 3 It / This
4 This / That 5 This / That

Exercise 3

1 b 2 a 3 a 4 b 5 a

Unit 5

Working with words

Exercise 1

1 c 2 b 3 a 4 c 5 b 6 a 7 c
8 b 9 c 10 c

Exercise 2

1 pay, to
2 thrives, on
3 steer, of
4 spurred, into
5 focus, on
6 cope, with
7 relied, on
8 deviate, from

Business communication

Exercise 1

1 I don't know if you are aware …
2 Look, can we try and avoid any …?
3 How do you propose we deal with this issue?
4 Can we try and stay focused on the facts?
5 The real issue here is …
6 Do you understand what I'm trying to say?
7 I see what you mean, but …
8 Let's try not to get personal here.
9 Can I just make sure I've understood this correctly?
10 I just don't understand how …

Exercise 2

1 if you are aware
2 I be right in thinking
3 just don't understand
4 prepared to
5 you be happy
6 a bit worried
7 what you mean
8 be more than happy
9 we try and avoid
10 not happy with

Language at work

Exercise 1

1 Only at the end did he contribute to the meeting. / Only at the end of the meeting did he contribute.
2 My main question she didn't even answer / wasn't even answered.
3 It's her lack of professionalism I can't stand.
4 What's impressive is his boundless enthusiasm.
5 The person who's the best listener in our meetings is Zoe.
6 It's absolutely vital that you inform me of matters like that.
7 Creativity (is what) I value above anything else.
8 It's his constant need to make stupid jokes (that) I don't like.

Exercise 2

1 The **reason** I say this is because if we miss this date, then we lose the contract.
2 **Which / That** is why you need to fill in this form properly.
3 How we explain this to the board **is the problem**.
4 It's last month's sales figures **which / that** concern me.
5 In **which / that** case, Alan, **can** I leave you to email the supplier?
6 **What** concerns me is the cost of the materials.
7 The price of labour **I'm prepared to accept**.
8 The thing that confuses me **is this number here**.
9 What I'd like **to** know is when you can send a replacement part.
10 What we **must** be clear about is that this process exists for a reason.

Unit 6

Working with words

Exercise 1

1	figure	6	fall
2	bounce	7	get
3	think	8	try
4	Look	9	run
5	hit	10	get

Exercise 2

1 e 2 b 3 d 4 g 5 a
6 f 7 c 8 h

Business communication

Exercise 1

1 I'm not sure how this would work in practice, but how about …?
2 I would have thought it would be possible to …
3 What makes you think that would work?
4 Thinking about it, we could even …
5 Would you like to expand on that?
6 Well, I just thought that in that way …
7 It's certainly worth thinking about.
8 Shouldn't we be thinking more about …?
9 I was thinking along the lines of …

Exercise 2

(Other answers are possible in some gaps.)
1 Couldn't we consider
2 Supposing we were to
3 Sorry, are you saying
4 so you're thinking
5 that's not such a bad idea
6 I'm concerned about
7 We should at least consider it

Language at work

Exercise 1

1 rather / quite
2 quite / rather
3 little
4 only
5 absolutely / quite
6 Even
7 quite / absolutely
8 all
9 just
10 actually

Exercise 2

(Other answers are possible in some gaps.)
1 quite / rather
2 absolutely / really / completely
3 honest
4 very / rather / quite / really
5 in fact / actually
6 even / quite
7 only / just
8 course
9 just
10 really
11 actually / definitely / easily

Unit 7

Working with words

Exercise 1

1 shared vision
2 structural change
3 collective aspiration
4 employee participation
5 performance management, personal development plans
6 paradigm shift
7 skills deficit

Exercise 2

across the board
get in the **real** world
in the long run
the **bigger** picture

Exercise 3

1	one-size-fits-all	5	top-down
2	centrally-driven	6	bottom-up
3	decentralized	7	generic
4	job-specific	8	self-directed

Business communication

Exercise 1

1 Could you clarify exactly what the problems were?
2 Do you mean that …
3 What I'm saying is …
4 What was the name of the other logistics company again?
5 Have you heard that Hans has handed in his notice?
6 By the way, talking about …
7 That's a bit of a digression.
8 Let's get back to the main issue.

Exercise 2

1	say	5	not
2	about	6	thought
3	by	7	doesn't
4	out		

Language at work

Exercise 1

(suggested answers only)
1 I was going to finish working on the Kelner case, but too many other things came up.
2 I was meeting Sue at 10.00 a.m., but she's off sick at the moment.
3 I was supposed to meet the Hungarian rep at 12.30 p.m. and take him for lunch, but his plane was delayed.
4 I was going to file my corporate credit card expenses, but I couldn't find my receipts.
5 I had intended to book flights for the Atlanta conference, but the airline's website kept crashing.
6 I was going to meet Sarah at Café Carlucci, but it was closed so we went to Spangio's instead.
7 I was going to check my bank account, but there's no point because we don't get paid until tomorrow.

Exercise 2

1 e 2 a 3 g 4 b 5 d 6 c 7 f

Unit 8

Working with words

Exercise 1

1	make, to	4	feel, of
2	gained, for	5	take, in
3	have, in	6	see, for

Exercise 2

1	provides, for	5	turn, into
2	takes pride, in	6	unites, in
3	provided, with	7	building, up
4	opened, up	8	striving, for

Business communication

Exercise 1

1 we are at the moment
2 just like to outline
3 it would be a good idea if I
4 the first thing is
5 a good point
6 remember exactly
7 I think you should be aware
8 have to admit that
9 I'll get back to you

Exercise 2
1 **I'd** like to …
2 … **we need to** address …
3 I don't have the **exact** figures …
4 I think this **is a really** / this **really is an** important point / I **really** think …
5 I can **double check** if you like?
6 I think that**'s covered** / that **covers** everything.
7 … I **still need to** / **still have to** run that by …

Language at work

Exercise 1
1 Would you say you have many weaknesses?
2 I'd like to know what attracted you to this position.
3 You're not unhappy in your present job, are you?
4 What salary are you looking for?
5 You must have some questions to ask us?

Exercise 2
1 a 2 b 3 a 4 b 5 a 6 b
7 b 8 b 9 a

Exercise 3
a 1,8 b 2,6 c 7 d 9 e 5

Unit 9

Working with words

Exercise 1
1 corporate accountability
2 track record
3 knowledge base
4 assets
5 bottom line
6 critical success factor
7 natural resources, sustainable development
8 endangered species

Exercise 2
1 cost-benefit analysis
2 drain on resources
3 short-term profit
4 return on investment
5 quantifiable data
6 market value
7 long-term viability

Business communication

Exercise 1
1 b 2 a 3 b 4 a 5 b 6 b
7 a 8 b

Exercise 2
1 provided we all work together
2 assuming we decided to hold
3 have to bear in mind the long-term viability
4 there's no point going ahead with this meeting if we don't
5 we need to develop a clear strategy
6 we don't have much choice
7 the general consensus is that

Language at work

Exercise 1
1 e 2 a 3 g 4 c 5 b 6 j 7 d
8 h 9 f 10 i

Exercise 2
1 If I **knew**
2 we **said / would say** so
3 **I'll be** amazed.
4 wouldn't **have** so many
5 **had** had a pay rise
6 If they **offered** you
7 I'**d** / I **would** vote
8 **if** LPGJ turn it down
9 Provided we **offer** to cover your relocation expenses, **will** you take the job?
10 If I **had been** reappointed

Unit 10

Working with words

Exercise 1
1 commitment
2 decisive
3 conviction
4 self-aware
5 people-focused
6 humble
7 collaborative
8 hands-off
9 adaptable
10 integrity
11 empathy
12 passionate
Hidden word = micromanages

Exercise 2
1 establish
2 instil
3 avoid
4 credibility
5 influence
6 generate
7 work together
8 culture of trust
9 sense of cohesion
10 be consistent in
11 recognize
12 reinforces

Business communication

Exercise 1
1 it has been agreed that
2 Apparently, the decision was taken
3 As I understand
4 what this will allow us to do is
5 Another great thing about this change is
6 my understanding
7 it will be well worth the inconvenience
8 the benefits are clear
9 you and your teams are crucial to
10 has a key role to play in
11 I would encourage all of you to

Exercise 2
(suggested answers only)
SH: This is something I wanted to bring up. **I like the idea of making** departments more accountable for their training budgets, **but I'm not very happy about** having to make choices between competing training needs that are equally valid. How do we ensure that essential training will still take place? **Can you give us an assurance that** this will be taken into consideration?
CJ: Well, of course, **that's a valid point, but** the difference is that at the moment the HR Department decides how much of the budget is spent on job-specific training, IT skills, language training, etc. In future, individual departments will be free to choose their own priorities. **My understanding is** that it should make everyone's lives easier, so **let's give this a chance to work**.

Language at work

Exercise 1
1 Five of our products were being sold every minute in 2017.
2 Having been asked to email us details, he didn't get back in touch with us.
3 You will be interviewed before you are allowed to register for work here.
4 The flowers might have been sent yesterday.
5 To have been selected was a great honour.
6 Your order was being processed when the whole system crashed.
7 A formal reply is going to be written to address your complaints.
8 15,000 orders have been received – a staggering number.

Exercise 2
1 had been more than made up for
2 put
3 were published
4 showed
5 were divided
6 was reinvested
7 paid out
8 went
9 was raised
10 Looking
11 to have been invited
12 to put in
13 to build
14 Having been voted
15 anticipate

Unit 11

Working with words

Exercise 1
1 Diversity
2 pioneering
3 responsibility
4 unity
5 merit, competence
6 Mutual cooperation
7 integrity
8 equality
9 tolerance
10 excellence
11 respect, dignity

Exercise 2
1 significantly
2 surprisingly
3 irretrievably
4 potentially
5 relatively
6 comparatively
7 irretrievably
8 potentially

Business communication

Exercise 1
1 beyond
2 stuck
3 possibly
4 firm
5 say to
6 out
7 way round

Exercise 2
1 reached, where
2 employing
3 just not
4 budge
5 along
6 in
7 do
8 would
9 to say

Exercise 3
A We're in a **very difficult** situation …
B … this idea about job-sharing **just won't** work.
B … consider **re-allocating** jobs and **redefining** roles instead?
A … I'd be willing **to hear** …
A … I have to say no to **redefining** roles …
B … that's **out** of the question …
A I suppose that **is feasible / sounds feasible / would be feasible / could be feasible / might be feasible**.
A **Are we all agreed / Do we all agree** that we need **to think** …

Language at work

Exercise 1
1 Having considered
2 Given
3 Faced with / Given
4 As changing / Knowing / Given
5 Offering
6 Knowing / Given
7 At no time
8 Under no circumstances / At no time
9 Not only

Exercise 2
1 Knowing that the train had been cancelled, I took the bus instead.
2 Given my disappointment in the quality, I won't buy from them again.
3 Having considered the choices available, I decided to go for this one.
4 Faced with the news going public, he had no option but to step down.
5 Offering them / the client a larger discount was the only way to keep the client / them.
6 As changing the deadline wasn't feasible, we decided to reduce the volume instead.
7 Under no circumstances must / should visitors go beyond the reception without a pass.
8 Not only do they offer a very generous pension scheme, (but) they also offer flexitime.
9 At no time have we failed to live up to our core values of decency, innovation and trust.

Unit 12

Working with words

Exercise 1
1 generate a demand
2 reinforce an association
3 play on
4 tailor
5 promote the consumption of

Exercise 2
1 across 2 to 3 into 4 in
5 up 6 up 7 out 8 into

Exercise 3
1 motivational
2 aspirational
3 market penetration
4 exploitative
5 status anxiety
6 USP
7 materialistic
8 consumer profiles

Business communication

Exercise 1
1 become apparent
2 comes across
3 first benefit
4 second point
5 having said
6 is achievable
7 strong position
8 Because we
9 very much
10 serious consideration

Exercise 2
1 c 2 f 3 a 4 e 5 b 6 d

Language at work

Exercise 1
1 Basically
2 obviously
3 Anyway
4 After all
5 Quite honestly
6 As a matter of fact
7 Admittedly
8 so to speak
9 Mind you
10 Of course
11 To tell you the truth

Exercise 2
1 b 2 a 3 b 4 b 5 a 6 a 7 b
8 a 9 a 10 b